T0118492

Four Years In Castro's Cuba

AN AMERICAN PRIEST'S EXPERIENCE 1994-1998

FR. PAT SULLIVAN O.F.M. CAP

authorHOUSE®

AuthorHouse™
1663 Liberty Drive
Bloomington, IN 47403
www.authorhouse.com
Phone: 1-800-839-8640

© 2012 by Fr. Pat Sullivan O.F.M. Cap. All rights reserved.

No part of this book may be reproduced, stored in a retrieval system, or transmitted by any means without the written permission of the author.

Published by AuthorHouse   06/22/2012

ISBN: 978-1-4772-1243-1 (sc)
ISBN: 978-1-4772-1244-8 (e)

Library of Congress Control Number: 2012909499

Any people depicted in stock imagery provided by Thinkstock are models, and such images are being used for illustrative purposes only.
Certain stock imagery © Thinkstock.

This book is printed on acid-free paper.

Because of the dynamic nature of the Internet, any web addresses or links contained in this book may have changed since publication and may no longer be valid. The views expressed in this work are solely those of the author and do not necessarily reflect the views of the publisher, and the publisher hereby disclaims any responsibility for them.

Preface

ALTHOUGH I SERVED as a Catholic pastor in Cuba from 1994 until 1998, it wasn't until around 2003 that I started writing down some of my experiences and thoughts, which came to form this little book. I approached a couple of publishers with it, but found no interest. So I made it available over the internet to anyone who might be interested in Cuba.

As now in 2012 my family has kindly offered to see about printing up a small number of copies, I wondered if some up-dating of the material should be done. After all, a number of years have passed. But while I have been interested in following the news about what has since happened in Cuba I am by no means an expert on more recent events. And as I have been serving the small Spanish-speaking community in Okinawa, Japan for the past seven years my access to Cuban news is limited. So, I just present here the text as it is: my view of the Cuban situation during the years I actually lived there.

Having moved from English to Spanish, then to Mískito in Nicaragua, then to Japanese, my grammar, spelling and capitalization practices have become a bit confused. I am grateful for the editing and correction help of my brother and of Prof. Anthony Jenkins of the Ryukyu University here in Okinawa, but I'll have to take responsibility for errors and inconsistencies that remain.

May God grant that these pages be of some use in promoting better understanding and peace among nations.

(March 3, 2012)

Fr. Pat Sullivan and Pope John Paul II during January 1998
Papal visit to Santa Clara, Cuba

Introduction

From 1994 until 1998 I had the pleasure of serving as Catholic pastor of two parishes in Cuba. I was the only American priest serving on the island. Both during my assignment there and after returning to the States (having been obliged to leave by the Cuban government) I have often been surprised to find how little even many well-educated Americans know about the real situation in Cuba. And it is not just a *lack* of information. Quite a few people have been *misinformed*, sometimes quite deliberately, about how things really are there.

The frequent misunderstanding of the Cuban reality is usually accompanied by an even further ignorance of the actual policies of the United States government regarding that country, especially concerning the economic embargo laws and the immigration policies as applied to Cubans.

For example, when I mention to people that I was personally warned by a U.S. State Department official that any Catholics in the States who would try to send me in Cuba more than $300 a month worth of free medical supplies for the sick of my parish without first getting a Treasury Department license would be subject to up to 10 years in Federal prison for "trading with the enemy", they think I am making it up or exaggerating.

So, I have decided to put down on paper some of my first-hand experiences as a parish priest in Cuba during those four years. I viewed the reality there through the lens of my being an American, and also of my previous 20 years of ministry in Honduras, Nicaragua, El Salvador and

Guatemala. I don't pretend to write as a historian, sociologist or political scientist. I would just like to share what I found there and what I lived there as a parish priest. And I would like in a small way to be a voice for the Cuban Catholics whom I came to love dearly there, as at present they have little chance of being able to speak freely for themselves.

I am somewhat nervous in trying to do this, because I am pretty sure that I will be bitterly attacked for whatever I say. The present government in Cuba and many of its supporters do not accept any criticism. They tend to interpret even the slightest negative commentary as just one more part of the imperialist conspiracy to crush the Cuban people. On the other hand, the fiercely anti-Castro people here in the States are often likewise enraged by *any* favorable comment about *anything* good the Communists have done there. To try to present a balanced and truthful description of the reality in Cuba is unacceptable to either extreme. I have more than once observed how the prayerfully thought out and carefully worded sermons of Cardinal Ortega in Havana are simultaneously denounced by the Cuban government as treason, and by the anti-Castro forces in the U.S. as abject surrender to Communism.

But as Jesus said: "The truth will make you free." Indeed, I recall that the longest and loudest applause that Pope John Paul II received during his visit to Cuba was when he quoted those words during his homily at his final out-door Mass in Havana.

What I am going to present in this book is true. However, I have to keep in mind that people I dearly love are still in Cuba, where the accusation of the "crime" of "cooperation with enemy propaganda" is used quite freely by the State Security forces, and the punishments can be harsh. So, I often have to delete names, dates, locations or other details that might bring repression on the individuals or groups involved. I look forward to the day when they will be able to speak freely for themselves and tell their story much better than I can.

1

Christmas in Cuba

WHEN I ARRIVED at the parish to which I had been assigned in Cuba in 1994, one of the most striking things was my first Christmas there, unlike any Christmas I had ever experienced elsewhere. In a sense you could say that the way Christmas is observed (or not observed) there says a lot about the situation of the people.

Many years before my arrival the government had abolished the public celebration of Christmas, supposedly in order not to interrupt the "zafra": the vital sugar cane harvest which is going on in December. In reality, of course, it was the overall policy of the Communist government to get people away from all religious belief and practice, in the expectation that religion would steadily and completely disappear in the light of Marxist thought. In any case when I got there Christmas was publicly just another normal work and school day: not a day off for anyone. Those who wished could attend church services before or after work or school, but outside the church buildings there was nothing. No decorations in the street, no sales in the stores, no Christmas programs or music on TV or radio. It fact it was forbidden even to make reference to the existence of Christmas on TV or radio. Once while I was there one of the evening news anchormen made the mistake of adlibbing "Christmas greetings to those who celebrate it" at the end of the Dec. 24 evening broadcast, and was promptly suspended.

In one sense I found it nice to have Christmas as a purely religious experience, free of all the gross commercialization that so damages the celebration in most countries. I was certainly glad to see a Christmas free from the ritual drunkenness that so often accompanies it. I remember when I was first studying Spanish at the Maryknoll language school in Cochabamba, Bolivia in 1974. I had learned enough Spanish to be able to celebrate Mass at the local parishes, and was asked to do the Midnight Mass on Christmas Eve at a downtown chapel. I was enjoying the late-night walk to the chapel in the pre-Christmas darkness. But as I got closer to the center of town I found the streets full of roaring drunks. On each street corner there were people with cases of hard liquor, selling it by the bottle. In Central America likewise the abuse of alcohol is often a tragic and blasphemous way of observing Christmas. One Christmas Eve in Nicaragua I accepted the invitation to accompany the local group of "Alcoholics Anonymous" who had the practice of spending all that night in their meeting hall, with their families, since it was the only way of protecting themselves from the constant invitations to "have a drink! It's Christmas!" So, it was nice to experience a sober Christmas in Cuba.

While Christmas in Cuba was celebrated only in church buildings, believers could also have a Christmas crib or decorations in their homes if they wished, as long as they were not visible from the street. If it was too visible, the local "Committee for the Defense of the Revolution" would pay a visit and let it be known that it was not acceptable.

At my parish the rectory and office were right next door to the church, and had large "French door" type shutters opening onto the park in front of the church. There was no glass, just iron bars. There we had the custom of setting up a big elaborate nativity scene inside each year, with dozens of painted plaster figures (by now much the worse for wear). It was quite visible from the park and street, but because it was inside a church building we could just barely get away with it. We decided to push the envelope and add some lights, and leave a tape recorder playing Christmas hymns. Many, many people would stop and stare, sometimes literally open-mouthed. There were, of course, the few believers who had never abandoned the public practice of their faith. There were also many drop-outs who had long ago submitted to the relentless pressure of official atheism, but felt guilty about it and still felt the longing for the things of the spirit. And there were the younger folk, raised from kindergarten as Marxist atheists but still possessing the natural longing for God. I used to enjoy watching the little kids who would spot the nativity lights from a block away and drag their parents over to see. "Look! Look! How pretty!"

As Christmas celebrates the reality of God who so loves us that He became human for us, it is really the heart of our faith. So it somehow survived in Cuba even when all the external trappings had been stripped away. Our Masses on Christmas Eve and Christmas Morning were deeply joyful, and attendance grew from year to year.

My second year there we pushed the envelope a bit further and put a Christmas star in lights way up on top of the bell tower, visible from far away. We waited, fully expecting the police to drop by and tell us to take it down, but no objection was raised. The parishioners were astonished.

As the government's tolerance toward religion grew in the 90's, more and more people started to recover a bit of Christmas. This put the Communists in a dilemma. They had to allow Christmas decorations in the tourist hotels and bars to keep the foreign visitors happy, but they didn't want them in any other public places. The more clever believers took advantage of the fact that January First is the celebration of the anniversary of the Revolution and Castro's triumphal entry into Havana after the fall of the Batista regime, and it is celebrated in a big way. So some "Christmas" decorations might be put up visibly, but claiming if challenged that they were really "Jan.1" decorations! And once the government "dollar stores" (which sell scarce goods only for dollars in cash) realized that there was a market, they started offering plastic Christmas trees, strings of lights, etc., all under the ruse of being "Jan.1" decorations, or decorations for the tourist trade. (Ironically, all the Christmas decorations on sale were made in—of course—Communist China.) Eventually the Party issued a decree officially declaring that the plastic evergreen tree was inherently a religious symbol, and hence could not be displayed in any public institution or on the street. In our Diocese the Bishop managed to run off some sheets of paper with the outlines of the nativity figures that people could cut out and color. The kids loved doing it and set them up at home.

I'll relate here the experience of a lady in a neighboring parish who was kind enough (and brave enough) to later share her story (and even allow it to be printed). She had grown up in a nominally Catholic family, but as a young woman she was totally swept up in the Revolution and came to full acceptance of Marxist doctrine, including atheism. She was content and enthusiastic about building a wonderful new society without God. She married a man of like ideas, and they were happily raising their kids as Marxist atheists. But one thing continued to bother her. Each year at Christmas time she would recall very pleasant memories of her girlhood Christmases. It saddened her to look at her little ones and know that they would never experience any of that. It bothered her so much for years that she finally decided to do something very foolish. As Christmas approached one year she decided to take the kids to a church to see the nativity scene. She was careful. She told them they were going shopping and got on a bus with them. She had decided to take them to the church farthest away from where they lived, in the hopes that no one would recognize her if they saw her go in with the kids. On the bus she even discreetly put on dark glasses and a scarf. They got off on the other side of town, and as they walked past the church she ducked inside, pulling the kids in after her. The kids were astonished! They had never been inside a church, and were fascinated by such a strange place. Then they spotted the nativity scene and ran over, enchanted by all the little statues. They were full of questions. "Mommy, who is that? . . . What are they doing? . . . Who are those people with wings? . . . What does it mean?" The woman had no choice but to try to answer their questions, as her own childhood memories flooded back. "That's the baby Jesus, who some people thought was God come to earth . . . That's Mary, his Mommy . . . Those are the shepherds, with their sheep and doggy, who went to worship him . . . Those are angels telling everyone Jesus was born . . . That's King Herod sending his soldiers to try to kill the baby . . ." She admitted later that her thoughts were very confused. As she answered their questions she was also saying to herself: "This is STUPID! I no longer BELIEVE any of this! . . . If the Party finds out I'm here I'll have problems at work! . . . If the kids' teachers find out they will target the kids for public ridicule for being superstitious! . . . My husband will be furious! . . . WHY am I doing this???" Yet she said that she really could not stop. Somehow, she HAD to tell them that story.

Well, she got the kids home, somehow convincing them on the way that they should never tell anyone where they had been or what they had seen, not even Daddy. But she herself could not stop thinking and questioning. She could have brushed it off as just a crazy attack of nostalgia, but she was too honest to do that. She thought, and she read, and she questioned, and finally she prayed. Eventually she returned fully to the Faith, resigned from the Communist Party, and finally became a very active Catechist in her parish.

In his novel "Brideshead Revisited" Evelyn Waugh borrows an image from G.K. Chesterton: that God is like a fisherman who uses an incredibly long line, incredibly thin. No matter how far away we swim, or how deep we dive, God has only to twitch the line to draw us back. Christmas was the part of the faith in Cuba that survived the harsh years of repression of religion, and in my years there I often saw Christmas drawing people back. Not the Christmas of piles of presents and abundance of food and drink, but the Christmas of God coming lovingly among us in poverty and humility.

On the occasion of the Pope's visit in 1998, Fidel allowed Christmas to again be a day off. Whether the change will be permanent remains to be seen. And what future Christmases will be like in Cuba is anybody's guess. I rather hope that a gift that the Cuban Church will offer the world will be a Christmas purified by persecution and reduced to its glowing heart of love. In any case, while I was there Christmas each year was a very important moment for the faithful to affirm their commitment, and for others to discover (or rediscover) Jesus.

2

"Solving Supper": Food in Cuba

WHEN I ARRIVED in Cuba in 1994 my knowledge of Spanish was already quite good, and after having spoken it for 20 years in Central America I thought that my vocabulary about food was pretty complete. One could cook (*cocinar*) supper, or prepare (*preparar*) it, but in Cuba I learned that one had to solve (*resolver*) supper, and breakfast and lunch as well. That meant that one had first to solve the problem of obtaining something to cook, then solve the problem of obtaining enough fuel to cook it with, then solve the problem of getting enough light to eat it by if the electricity was out again. All this took creativity, patience and time each day. I never encountered cases of starvation or malnutrition such as I had seen in Central America, but the effort to obtain enough food in Cuba was constant.

On paper the Communist system looked fine. Every household had a ration book, counting how many people were in each household and their condition. Each home was assigned to a particular State grocery shop where one could pick up all the necessities at a low subsidized price. The State would keep the grocery shops stocked because the State owned or controlled all agriculture and means of production and distribution.

In reality, because the State did not usually pay the farmers and other workers enough really to stimulate and reward good production and distribution of produce, food was always somewhat scarce. You would always get something at the shop, but rarely the amount the ration book said you were supposed to get, and something was always missing. So for what was lacking one had to use the illegal black market, or go to one of the limited "free" markets. The "free" markets were a recent innovation which allowed farmers to sell at supply-and-demand prices whatever they produced in excess of their quota that they had sold to the State. The prices, of course, were much higher at the "free" markets, and the hard-core Communists hated them as being a surrender to capitalism, but they made some food available.

Our rectory was a "household", so we had our ration book which we were required to keep up to date at the local control office according to exactly how many priests or religious actually lived there. For most of my four years in Cuba I was alone, so I was a one-person household. Fortunately for me a nice lady down the street did me the kindness of keeping my ration book for me and picking up my food when she picked up her family's, saving me a lot of time waiting in line. In gratitude I let her keep what I didn't want. The ration book is complete. You get a certain number of cigars and cigarettes at low subsidized price whether you smoke or not, and a set quantity of low quality rum whether you drink or not, a small portion of soap, etc. So, I let her keep my tobacco and rum. Not that she smoked or drank it. It could be easily bartered. Find someone who would rather smoke than eat cabbage and you had some extra food for the week. Find someone who would rather drink than wash and you had yourself an extra fragment of soap. I used to meet once a week with a wonderful elderly Cuban gentleman. He was a retired English teacher, and still managed to earn a little giving private classes. We would meet weekly so he could practice his English and clear up questions. Sometimes he would bring along other teachers or students to practice English conversation. I recall his great joy when on the occasion of Fidel's birthday everyone was granted a special ration of four bottles of beer. He was so glad to swap his beer for someone else's soap, because cleanliness was so important to his self-esteem.

Bread was similarly rationed. My helpful friend would pick up my one-person chunk (about 3 inches) at our assigned State bakery each afternoon, and I would save it for breakfast the next day. (It was customary that the person who stood in line at the bakery for the family be allowed to break off the end of the loaf to munch on the way home.)

The meat ration was small and irregular, and usually consisted of ground meat of undetermined origin, heavily mixed with soy or other grain (*picadillo*). I found it quite delicious. Eggs and fish were likewise included sporadically.

Pregnant women and nursing mothers got extra rations, and small children were guaranteed daily rations of milk or yogurt. (The kids' milk ration was considered so sacred by the State that the government would spend considerable amounts of scarce hard currency to import powdered milk to make up for what was not produced locally.)

Families who had an elderly grandparent living with them considered themselves fortunate, because they were the ones to line up patiently for the rations. I was freed from a lot of these difficulties because the parishioners were very grateful to have me with them and would look after me, and make sure one way or another that I had enough to eat.

While I was there, the "free" markets became more and more important, even though their prices were high. The government began to allow them on a large scale after being terrified by the brief street riots in Havana in 1994. At first the police investigated thoroughly, looking for the ring-leaders who had planned and instigated the disturbances. When they finally realized that nobody planned them, but that they were spontaneous outbursts of pent-up frustration, they knew that something had to be done fast to get more food onto the markets.

But the black market was always another alternative. I was often told that the reason that Cuba, despite its rich land, could not produce enough milk to fulfill the ration plan was that so many milk cows were illegally slaughtered at night for the meat. Again, the Communist system can sound good in some ways, but when YOU own the cow you tend to protect and care for it. But when the State ("the people") own the cow and your ideals are weak, you just might look the other way when the cow disappears and you get some cash and some meat. There are many people in jail for illegal slaughter. (The story is often told—I can't vouch for its veracity—that when the local night train hit a cow on the tracks the train stopped to await the police. But when the cops got there they found only the horns, and many innocent-looking passengers with a little something extra—and bloody—stashed in their bags and under the seats.)

It is illegal for a Cuban to possess a lobster or a shrimp. The entire catch must be sold to the State in order to be resold for export or the tourist trade in order to bring in hard currency. The State needs hard currency in order to import medicines and other things not produced locally. The fishermen and divers don't enjoy turning over their entire catch for low prices. So if you look like you have money, you may be approached on the street by guys whispering "lobster? shrimp?". For the right price and with the right connections almost anything can be purchased on the black market.

For the purchase of prepared foods, the State restaurants usually had little selection and notoriously poor service. The local joke on rating restaurants is that if it is even open it gets one star. If it is open and actually has some food to sell it gets two stars. If the food is something that you actually want to eat, it gets three stars. If the waiting line is short enough so that you can get in before they run out of food, four stars. Five stars exist only in heaven. In recent years the State has responded to these deficiencies by licensing families to open their homes as private restaurants called *paladares*, as long as they have no more than twelve seats and have no non-family employees. They quickly became smashing successes for the quality of the cooking and service. But then to survive they would often have to resort to the black market to get the food to prepare, and then pay crushing taxes once they showed signs of success. Home pizza sellers were likewise licensed, to great popularity. The pizza was really just hot bread with a light sprinkling of oil and some sort of cheese, but lines would form as soon as they would start selling from the front window.

People learn to get by. They learn to solve each problem as it comes along. In the parish the "Christian Family Group" and the "Youth Group" would sometimes manage to put on a festive meal, pooling their resources for a modest smorgasbord (*mesa sueca*—"Swedish table"). Once everyone had brought their contribution to the common table, the organizers would count heads and prepare the exact number of plates so that everyone would get some. No "help yourself" and no seconds, but a little for everyone and the joy of sharing. For special celebrations they would pool part of their sugar rations weeks in advance and collect any kind of fruit available. The fruit juice and sugar would be mixed and allowed to ferment into something resembling wine in time for the party. (Yes, that's right: even sugar, produced by the millions of tons in Cuba, is rationed. The people joke that if Saudi Arabia ever goes Communist the first thing that will happen will be the rationing of sand.)

Cakes can be bought from the State bakery under controlled conditions. If you present your ID proving you have a birthday coming up, you can negotiate a birthday cake. Special occasions can sometimes merit a cake. Religious celebrations never merit a cake. First Communion cakes were indeed sometimes obtained for the parish celebration for the kids, but silence and a smile were the only answer to my question "how on earth did you manage to get a cake for the First Communion kids?" Better not to know. On Mothers' Day the State went to considerable expense to provide a modest piece of cake for each household, its size proportionate to the number of names on the ration book. As it was presumed that every household had a mother of some sort, I likewise got my one-person Mothers' Day cake each year (which I wolfed down without guilt.) Celibate households do not fit in with the Marxist master plan.

Private vegetable gardens were sometimes encouraged, sometimes condemned, according to the ups and downs of Marxist theory. One of my chapels had a small walled-in enclosure along one side, and some of the women who regularly attended Mass decided to plant a small vegetable patch there. The harvest would mostly be given to some sick elderly people in the neighborhood, with the gardeners keeping a bit for themselves. So they cleared the ground, fertilized, (horse manure from the horse-drawn city "buses" of Santa Clara is carefully collected and is a hot commodity on the gray market), planted, watered and weeded. But as harvest drew near the local authorities dropped in to congratulate the ladies on their initiative, and to remind them that the entire harvest had to be turned over to the State at a price set by the State to be distributed by the State. End of project, and the land lay barren again from then on.

In recent years, as I noted, the State has opened up many "dollar stores" where food, clothing, soap, appliances, etc. can be bought for dollars in cash. This was quite a turn-around, as only a few years earlier the mere possession of dollars was a criminal offense. But the State needed to get hold of the dollars coming in from relatives abroad, or from tourist tips. So those with dollars could buy canned and packaged foods (sometimes even frozen meat), sodas, liquor, shoes, clothing, light bulbs, etc. there. This established two classes in a previously almost classless society: those with dollars and those with only Cuban pesos. I found myself torn. I wanted to be one of the people and share their situation. And as a Franciscan I was committed to voluntary and joyful poverty. But as a foreigner I did have some dollars. So I compromised and sometimes bought food there that couldn't be found elsewhere (cooking oil, canned meat, sardines, coffee, etc.) I also sometimes just cheated and splurged on a can of soda or some candy, feeling somewhat guilty. I remember once when I was taking the six-hour train ride to Havana from Santa Clara. Usually there was no food or drink available on the train or at the stations at that time. So I made myself a sandwich to bring along, and bought a dollars-only can of soda for 35 cents American to drink with it. But I ended up getting a seat with two other guys, facing a seat with three others. And as I got thirsty I also realized that the cost of that can of soda in dollars was the equivalent of about half a day's pay in pesos for those guys. So, I was too embarrassed to even take it out. It would have been like sipping champagne on a New York subway.

During my last years there the authorities began to allow a limited sale of "free market" food and drink to train passengers by wandering vendors at the stations. Previously that had been entirely forbidden as capitalist contamination. Once one of our friars, a native of Guatemala, was visiting Cuba to see how things were, and took a train ride to Santa Clara. In Central America whenever a bus or train stops (or slows down) it is surrounded by vendors offering all sorts of food and drink for sale to the passengers. But in Cuba when the train stopped at that time and a couple of illegal black market food vendors slipped out of the bushes to make some money selling to the passengers the police closed in to arrest them. When they ran, one of the cops foolishly fired a shot in the air to make them halt (Cuban cops very rarely use their guns—only in extreme situations). The Guatemalan friar was shocked, and his somewhat utopian vision of Cuba was severely tarnished from then on.

As in all things, the Cubans had a multitude of jokes about all this: that the favorite Cuban dish used to be "beans and rice", but Fidel had decided to change it to "beans or rice"; that *arroz con pollo* (rice with pieces of chicken cooked in it) had become *arroz con suerte* (rice with luck) because you were very lucky if you discovered a piece of chicken in your rice. I remember once a large gathering of lay parish leaders at the Bishop's house. Lunch was served, and it included a bowl of chicken soup. At first hardly anyone wanted the soup, until word spread that someone had actually found a sliver of chicken in her bowl! Unheard of!

But between all the difficulties in getting enough food, and all the jokes people made about it, and all the strategies to try to outwit the system, there is still a very important reality that should be recognized: the Cuban government is totally committed to the principle that food is a basic human right and that it is the solemn obligation of the Communist State to make sure that everyone has enough to eat. The methods they have chosen to try to achieve that goal often have not worked out successfully. Some Communists think that this can be remedied by including a limited amount of free market agriculture and productivity incentives to the over-all communist system. Others firmly proclaim that the pure Communist system would work perfectly if it weren't for the harmful effects of more than forty years of brutal economic embargo from the

United States, and the sudden withdrawal of aid from the collapsed Soviet Union. In any case, they try. Is the resulting shortage, shared by all, a worse situation than the starvation of the poor and the wasteful abundance of the rich found in some other Latin American countries? I wonder how many of the peasant farmers I knew in Central America would give up their economic "freedom" in return for a ration book that would guarantee that their kids would never go hungry, even though they would never get fat. When I compare the happy, well-fed, healthy, educated kids I knew in Cuba with so many sick and malnourished youngsters I have seen in Honduras, El Salvador, Nicaragua and Guatemala I make my observations on the deficiencies of the Cuban system with great respect for their good intentions, and great hope for their eventual success in guaranteeing food for all.

I should also add that as an American, I feel deeply ashamed that the U.S. trade embargo laws against Cuba have in practice prohibited or made difficult the sale of food and medicine to Cuba. Thanks to the efforts of some heroic members of Congress in Washington there are now some small exceptions to this, but for over 40 years we Americans have systematically tried to make sure that there *would be* shortages of food and medicine in Cuba, all in the name of anti-communism. We consider using hunger and disease as a weapon against civilians to be a crime against humanity when other people do it, but it seems not to bother us when we do it.

3

"Our Lady of the Swamp"
Religious Freedom and
Religious Repression

IN 1997 THE parish members who regularly attended Mass at the Cathedral in Santa Clara in central Cuba were told by the pastor that they would have to go to other neighboring parishes for a couple of weeks because the Cathedral would be closed for a little while for repairs and repainting. They were more than happy to do so, looking forward to having their Cathedral all fixed up nicely. But when they returned on the first Sunday that it was reopened they were astonished and delighted to find standing just inside the main doors a huge 12-foot-tall marble statue of the Virgin Mary, securely placed on a newly-installed concrete base. The older parishioners recognized the statue, despite the deep gouges and chips, and the dark stains here and there, and were happy to tell the younger people the story.

In the late 50's, shortly before the revolution which would put Fidel Castro in power, a beautiful marble statue of Mary had been purchased and installed in the center of a major traffic circle of the city of Santa Clara. The Catholic majority was delighted with it, (the Protestant minority less so.) But in the early 60's the revolution was channeled into totally Marxist lines, and the revolutionaries who were not in agreement were eliminated or suppressed. Atheism was an important part of the system, and while religion was not forbidden, a series of policies was put into place to make religious belief and practice more and more difficult. In that atmosphere the people woke up one morning to find that the huge statue of Mary had disappeared!

Although it weighed more than three tons and was impossible to move without major equipment, the government denied knowing anything about it and the case was closed.

Many years later the municipal government decided to expand one of the marketplaces by filling in the adjoining swampy area. All went fine until the bulldozer hit something solid in the mud. After much grinding, pushing and digging, the statue of Mary was partially uncovered. It had been dumped in the swamp and had submerged in the mud. The government didn't know what to do with it. But soon the authorities noticed that people were sometimes gathering there to pray, leaving lighted candles at times. So once again the statue disappeared during the night and once again the government (the only owner of cranes and moving equipment) denied knowing anything. More years passed, with occasional rumors of the statue having been seen stashed here and there.

But in the 90's the Cuban Communist Party began seriously to reevaluate its stance concerning religion. The repression against religion eased up, and the Party even publicly changed its statutes to allow religious believers to become members. The new official stance became that there was no intrinsic contradiction between revolutionary progress and religion.

Within this process Party officials quietly approached the Bishop of Santa Clara, admitting that the removal of the statue had been a mistake due to an excess of Marxist zeal. They said that it should at least have been respected as part of the artistic patrimony of the country. At the same time, they were not about to humiliate themselves publicly. So the understanding was reached: the government would clean and repair the statue and return it, but the Church would not put it outside, nor make a big stink about it. In complete secrecy the Bishop included the installation of a concrete base in the plans for the renovation of the Cathedral, and the government allowed the Church to get the needed materials. Once again the statue was moved in the dark of night, but this time to the vestibule of the Cathedral where the people joyously found it the next day. The Bishop refrained in his sermons from casting any blame. "She was gone, now she's back." He did insist, however, that the statue only be cleaned on the surface, but not repaired. The dents and gouges from the moving chains, and the deeper stains from the mud were retained as a silent testimony to history. As always, the Cubans could find some humor in it all. "Our Lady of the Swamp" ("*La Virgen de la Charca*") is a title not found in the liturgy books, but the Catholics there say it with a smile.

The story, I think, sums up what has happened in Cuba. In the earlier decades ('60's, '70's, into the '80's) it was the policy to try to make religious belief and practice disappear. They were careful never legally to prohibit religious belief and practice, lest they be accused of persecution of religion, but all sorts of things were done to make sure that people knew that religious belief would be a major problem for them in schools, places of work, and society in general. Then in the '90's there were major changes in the thinking of some (but not all) Party leaders, and toleration of religion has been growing steadily. It is far from complete, but much progress has been made compared to the early years.

Here once again it is difficult truthfully to describe the reality I knew during those four years in Cuba without being blasted from both sides.

The Communists, while now being more tolerant, will generally deny totally in public that there has ever been anything which could be called religious persecution or repression (and manage to do it with a straight face.) The extreme anti-Castro forces on the other hand will usually deny that any progress has been made. They will generally speak only of the worst years of repression, and consider any recognition that changes or progress have been made as being surrender to Communism.

I recall the day in early 1998 when the Pope arrived in Cuba. (I'll devote a separate chapter to those tremendous days.) I had the TV on in the parish meeting room (everything was broadcast live and uncensored nation-wide) and about 20 or 30 parishioners were gathered to watch together, sitting on the plastic chairs. The instant the plane's wheels touched down there was cheering, applause and weeping from almost all. He's here! We are not alone! I had tears in my eyes as well. The joy continued as the plane stopped and the Pope got out. Then came the moment when Fidel stood up to make his speech of welcome. I hoped that the security forces did not have any *orejas* ("ears": undercover spies) among us that day. Expressions of disgust and loathing. "How DARE he put on such a show after all he has done to us!" Some walked out and would only return when the Pope would speak. The man sitting next to me, usually a quiet fellow who never spoke much, turned to me trembling with rage. He poured out the story of when he was a kid. His family was one of the few that continued to practice the faith publicly in the years of anti-religious repression. There were a couple of kids like himself who were taking religion classes in preparation for the Sacrament of Confirmation. The date was set (a Sunday) when the Bishop would come and Confirm the little group. But the school teachers worked in coordination with the police and with the local Committees for the Defense of the Revolution. When they knew that a student was taking religion classes, they would often ridicule him or her in class, and encourage the other kids to do likewise. So when they heard the date set for the Confirmation, they announced a couple of days before that on that Sunday there would be a special sports day, and attendance was obligatory. (This was a regular tactic.) But this kid was all enthused to be confirmed, so he skipped the sports day and went to his Confirmation Mass. On Monday he was told that he was left back and would have to repeat the entire school year despite his excellent marks. Decades later the wound still hurt.

The testimonies are numerous, far too numerous and consistent to have been made up as anti-Castro propaganda. Again and again people shared their experiences of what would happen if you even went to Mass regularly: harassment in school, denial of university admittance or of degrees, loss of promotion at work, mockery on the street, denial of access to any political influence (since the only Party would not accept believers). And of course the confiscation of all Catholic schools; the prohibition of all religious radio and television programs; the restriction on religious literature, publications or Bibles; the prohibition of processions or public religious acts outside of churches; the restrictions on repair of churches, on obtaining cars for church use, etc. etc.

But that had changed considerably by the time I arrived in Cuba in 1994, and continued to change during my four years there. During my first weeks there I accompanied the pastor whom I was going to replace (a fellow Capuchin Friar, from Guatemala) to the local Communist Party headquarters for a meeting with the official in charge of "Religious Affairs". (We had to deal with that office a lot, as they had absolute power.) He was a friendly atheist, somewhat well-read regarding Christianity. He explained that he had received new instructions. It was now part of his job to accept complaints from workers who believed that they had been discriminated against at work because of their religious belief, and to intervene with the managers to insist that all workers be treated fairly and that their religious status not be a factor in promotions or work placements. Quite a change.

Likewise the many kids and teens who came to church for religious instruction on Saturdays and Sundays did so rather freely, and very rarely told of having any trouble with their teachers on that account. Only a few years before they came to the religion classes by discreetly slipping through a small side door lest they be noticed. Now they poured in and out of the wide-open main door, sometimes inviting their friends to come along.

During the week we would usually have the church doors open most of the afternoon. My church opened right onto a little park, and the school kids (all in revolutionary red shorts and skirts) would go to the park for recess and games. Many would slip into the church to say a prayer or to just explore. The teachers who were believers (in public or in private) would be happy to look the other way. But I remember that once another teacher got upset and went in to round up her errant kids and herd them out, telling them they should not enter the church. They were quite obedient, so they stayed outside and knelt down on the church steps to pray. Their teacher, exasperated, gave up the battle. Another time I happened to be standing outside the church when a teacher was marching her class someplace, all uniformed and lined up two-by-two. When the kids who go to religion class spotted me they broke ranks to run up and give me a kiss (Cuban kids are very affectionate) calling out "El Padre! El Padre!" Teacher was not amused.

By the time the Cuban government obliged me to leave in 1998 I would say that in general most Cubans could publicly express and practice religious faith without harassment, although with restrictions. There were still exceptions. Police officers and career army officers and their immediate families could not. Not that it was against the law for them. But they would be considered "security risks", and their careers would suffer. I recall once when a female army officer came to ask me to go with her to the military hospital where her father was awaiting death and wished to see a priest. She wanted to respect his wishes. When we got to the gate, at night, she tried just to walk me through with her (she was in uniform) but the guard stopped us for identification. She seemed to be torn. She wanted to carry out her father's request, was sad at his impending death, yet now probably had also the sinking feeling that if the guard reported that she had brought a priest in, her career would go down the tubes. The visit went well. Whether or not anything happened to her later I don't know. Likewise on those occasions when the parish had some copies of the Bible or New Testament available I was approached a few times by people who asked for a copy for a friend in the military who believed but was keeping it a secret. To be honest, I must admit that the Army Command has a good point: "How could we entrust the defense of Cuba against possible invasion to officers who claim to believe that one should turn the other cheek if struck, and love one's enemies? Christians, if they practice what they believe, would be terrible soldiers."

On the university level, tolerance toward religion had much improved. There was even a recognized group of "Christian University Students" who managed to hold public and respectful dialogues on the subject of religion with the "Communist Youth" group. I was told, however, that believers were still automatically excluded from some courses of study such as psychology, sociology and political science, and religious discrimination was still in force in some areas of education. I recall talking with a high-school girl who was very active in the parish youth group. An outstanding student, she had been picked for an exceptionally good university program. But on the form to be filled out there was still the simple question : "Do you belong to any church or religious group?", with space for just a "yes" or "no". Although it was not stated anywhere, everyone knew that a "yes" on that question would end the process, and she would be shunted to a lesser-ranked college. But she really loved Jesus and the Church. Her family urged her to just lie and keep her faith inside. She did, and it broke her heart.

So, it was still a mixed bag as far as tolerance for religion went, but I believe it is important to point out that much progress has been made. When I talk to people here in the States, they sometimes ask me if there are any churches open in Cuba, or if I could celebrate Mass there. When I describe the full churches and thriving parishes they are often quite surprised, as they had the impression of a brutal persecution there.

Before leaving the topic of religious freedom and religious repression in Cuba, it might be well to see things in a broader context. Fidel is a brilliant orator, in my opinion. He is at his best when he deflects criticism of his regime by pointing out the failings of other regimes. I have heard him say in speeches, "They say that Cuba does not respect religion. So I ask: 'How many bishops and priests have been shot in Cuba, and how many have been shot in El Salvador, that 'free' country which receives millions of dollars in arms from the United States? How many nuns have been raped, tortured or killed by soldiers and police officers in Cuba, and how many have been raped, tortured or killed by soldiers and police officers in the 'free democratic' countries of Central America? Such horrors have never happened in Revolutionary Cuba! Yet they denounce *us* for religious persecution!" A good point. People in the States ask me if I felt safe in Cuba. I answer honestly that I felt safer there than I feel in New York, and a great deal safer than in Central America. I like to maintain some eye contact with the people while I celebrate Mass. But for a time it was difficult in Central America. While I was serving as pastor in the city of Santa Tecla in El Salvador in 1992 a man came to the parish office one day to tell me that if I did not leave the country within ten days, they would kill me. Such threats were not uncommon, and a number of priests and bishops had already been shot, some while celebrating Mass. But we had decided to keep working despite the threats. When I informed the Archbishop he sent two of his lay legal aid workers to gather the details of the threat, and they were so used to such tasks that they had a form to fill out. As it happened, the threat was not carried out, although one unsuccessful kidnapping attempt was made, and I continued there for three years. But it was a challenge to look up at Mass to say, "The Lord be with you" to the people and at the same time be scanning the back doors for the sniper, and the pews for the face of the one who delivered the threat. It was likewise not comforting to know that the killer would probably have been trained and armed with U.S. tax-payers' money in the name of "freedom". In Cuba I had no fear of violence, and I could look the people in the face at Mass without flinching.

So, the acts of religious persecution that have been committed, and sometimes still are committed, in Cuba should be honestly faced and denounced. But the real progress that has been made (and I hope will continue to be made) toward complete religious freedom in Cuba should also be recognized, praised and encouraged. And while doing this we should not forget the brutal anti-religious actions committed in Central America by people supported, trained, armed and financed by us Americans. People who live in glass houses should not throw stones.

4

Going to Mass in Cuba

So, just what was parish life like there on a day-to-day basis? As I mentioned in the previous chapter, many people I talk to in the States are surprised to learn that Catholic churches are even open in Cuba, much less that they are doing well. The past and present reports of religious persecution in Cuba have gotten lots of publicity. The improvements in religious toleration over the last decade have gotten a lot less attention. I suspect that this was quite deliberate.

In Cuba, in the City of Santa Clara, I was Pastor of two adjoining urban parishes at the same time: "Mother of the Divine Shepherd" (commonly called simply "La Pastora"—"The Shepherdess"), and St. Anne. There was also a substantial sub-chapel of Holy Cross. I was the only priest. Until our Capuchin-Franciscan friars arrived from Central America to help in the early '90's, there had been no resident priest there for more than 20 years, but priests from other parishes would visit to celebrate Mass for the handful of people who persevered during the harsh years. The government's policy was one of not touching any church so long as it was still being used for services, even if only five people went. But if services stopped entirely, the building could be confiscated. (One of our heroic Spanish Capuchins succeeded in keeping the huge "Jesus de Miramar" Church in Havana open for decades, celebrating for a few faithful and supporting himself by raising a small herd of goats on the church property. It is now once again a thriving parish with a very active youth group.) We also had a rectory, office, and small meeting room in a building attached to the Pastora Church, although the larger three-story parish school and center had been taken over by the government and a wall built cutting our yard in half and between the two.

The center of parish life, there as everywhere in the world, was the celebration of the Eucharist—the Lord's Supper, the "Mass". In order to get to everyone I would celebrate two Masses on Saturday at two different places, and then have three Sunday Masses at the larger Pastora Church. The number of people attending was growing steadily. The old-timers could remember Sundays when fewer than a dozen people would be the total Sunday attendance. By the time I arrived in '94 the number had grown substantially, and when I left in '98 there were about 500 and the number was still growing.

I think I could truthfully divide those coming to mass into about seven different groups:

FIRST: The *"Truly Faithful"*: Those who had never given up the public practice of the Faith. They had endured criticism, ridicule, job problems and even the occasional threat or thrown rock, but had persevered with great courage and devotion.

SECOND: The *"Returned"*: This was the large group of people who had dropped out during the harsher years of religious repression. Some had simply hidden their faith in their hearts. Others had publicly renounced their beliefs and declared themselves atheists in order to get ahead, but had never really given up entirely. It was very beautiful to work with them. Often they would return rather ashamed of having given in. And often they were quite astonished to be welcomed home again and to be offered loving forgiveness and understanding. I remember once when the Sunday Gospel reading was the story of the "Prodigal Son" who had left his loving father and misspent all his inheritance. But when he repented and went back home his father rushed out to embrace and kiss him, so happy that his lost son was back. When the people sat down after that reading and I looked up to begin my sermon I realized that not much commentary was needed. Many were already drying their tears. That story was theirs. And likewise that part about the faithful brother who had never left, but resented his sinful brother's return. It was not always easy for the truly faithful to welcome back those who had strayed, especially those who had taken part in denouncing their neighbors for counter-revolutionary activity.

That wonderful process of return was still going on while I was there. The example of one person would get someone else to start thinking as well. There was a man in a neighboring parish who related his experience. He had wiped religion pretty well out of his mind. But one day the government truck in which he was riding had a flat tire. There was no spare, so he stayed with the truck while another worker went for one. But they happened to get the flat right next to a church, and that afternoon a group of ladies were gathered inside and were singing some of the old hymns to the Virgin Mary. As he listened he remembered how he and his family had sung those same tunes when he was a kid, and suddenly he found himself crying. That was all it took to break through the wall he had constructed in his mind. He went in and asked for something to read about Jesus, and eventually returned to the Church.

THIRD: The *"New Believers"*: This was the large and steadily growing group of younger people who had been raised as atheists since kindergarten. It had been drummed into them at home and at school that God did not exist and that all religion was destructive and foolish. But spiritual hunger cannot be denied forever. They questioned, they searched, and many eventually embraced the Faith. I won't deny that other factors may have been at work as well. Disillusionment with a failed or badly bruised vision of a Marxist paradise on earth can lead one to look elsewhere, anywhere, for something to fill the longing for an ideal by which to live. And of course it may be embedded in the genes of teenagers to have to do something to drive their parents nuts. So if your parents and teachers are dedicated Marxists, the best way to drive them up the wall is to wear a cross ("You can't go out of the house dressed like THAT, young lady!") or carry a bible or go to a church. If you want to be perceived by your friends as cool, wild, rebellious, cutting-edge: go to church on Sunday. It's one of the dangerous places your folks warned you to stay away from.

FOURTH: The *"Curious"*: With the increase of State religious toleration, a lot of people who never really gave much thought at all to religion suddenly found that there was an area of life totally unexplored. At any Mass there would be people who did not yet believe in any religion, but were very curious to see what all this was about. I found that it was very helpful at Mass often to pause and offer some explanation of what we were doing, and why, because there were always some present who didn't have a clue as to what was going on, but just liked being there.

FIFTH: The *"Reformers"*: I use this term for the many people who are deeply dissatisfied with Communism as it is lived today in Cuba. Some want only to modify the system. Others dream of a complete over-haul and full democratization. But they have very little space in Cuban society to even explore such ideas, much less speak or act on them. But they find the Church today to be a place where some new and challenging ideas are expressed, even if guardedly. I recall one such person telling me quite honestly: "I don't believe, but I go to Mass every Sunday because it is the only place in Cuba where people sometimes tell the truth." Here in the States if I announce at Mass that I will read even a half-page letter from the Bishops about the current national situation, I can hope at best for a yawn, if not a quiet stampede to the doors. In Cuba when I would announce that we would be reading a four-page letter from the Bishops, you could hear a pin drop. While critics sometimes say that the Cuban Bishops should be more outspoken, even what they do say regularly in their public statements and letters is often the strongest, and sometimes the only, public criticism of the Communist system. People listen with great attention, and wonder afterwards if the Bishop will be arrested for what was said.

SIXTH: The *"Santeros"*: When the African slaves were brought to Cuba, in huge numbers, they were not allowed to practice their old religions publicly. The Catholic Church was the only legal Church. (Protestantism was likewise quite illegal). But they were smart and they were survivors. They looked at the Spanish expressions of Catholicism and picked out anything that could resemble the divinities of their religion and made the connection. The Catholic use of statues and the veneration of Saints was a God-send for them. So the slaves could show great devotion to "Our Lady of Charity of Cobre", knowing that it was really the goddess Ochún in a Spanish gown. St. Barbara was really Changó, and poor Lazarus with the dogs licking his sores was really Babalú-Ayé. For some, the ideas became, over the years, quite mixed. And the "Babalaos", the spiritual leaders of the various Afro-Cuban religions, while they have their own beliefs and practices also hold the Catholic rites in great respect. Going to a Catholic Mass, or being baptized by a Catholic priest, can even be a requirement in order to advance to special Afro-Cuban rites. *Genuine* holy water, blessed by a real Catholic priest, was a required ingredient in some potions mixed by the Babalaos. So I would take into account that not all those devoutly attending Mass believed exactly what I do.

SEVENTH: The *"Orejas"* ("ears"): It had to be presumed that at any Mass, and especially at more important celebrations, there would be a number of "Ears", either plain-clothes police or trusted informants who were there in order to make a full report later as to all that had been said and as to who was present. I would sometimes explicitly welcome them in the introduction to the Mass, expressing the hope that they would learn something helpful, and the people would have a laugh at their expense.

So with folks from all seven categories present at Mass we had quite an interesting mix of people. We had some good choirs. Musical talent is spotted early in Cuba, and kids who show promise are placed in special music programs early on. This has produced a number of great world-class Cuban musicians, singers, dancers, etc. So we had some very talented musical people helping at the Masses. (I remember once at Mass noticing a couple of kids who were expertly playing the hymns that they heard on an imaginary keyboard on the pew in front of them. They were expert pianists while still in grammar school.)

The Pastora Church was in poor shape physically. There were large holes and gaps in the roof (not leaks, holes). When it rained during Mass we would have to look for a dry spot to shift the altar to, and people defended themselves from the rain as best they could. While the Communist government would carefully maintain Colonial churches if they were of great artistic or historical value, we had a hard time repairing other churches. Since the government controls the sale and distribution of all building materials, its good will and permission was needed for even the most minor repair. We had received a generous donation from the German Catholic Church to repair the roof, but even with the cash in hand it took about six years before we could actually buy materials. In the meantime, the black market was the only source available. In a sense this suited the Communists well. They knew we had gotten building materials on the black market, and we knew they knew. So in every conversation with them it was understood that they could walk in at any time and arrest us for illegal possession of cement. They didn't, but it was another handy club to keep over our heads.

The electricity would fail quite frequently. Even candles were very hard to obtain, so some night Masses were quite dark. Some people had flashlights, but nobody could obtain batteries for them. Eventually the "dollar stores" sold some re-chargeable Chinese electric lanterns which were a great help in church.

When I first arrived, it was still the custom to keep the large main doors of the church closed. during all Masses, especially Sunday morning. This was partly so that those who came to Mass could discreetly slip in and out by the small side doors so as to not attract attention. The people also remembered incidents in the past when enthusiastic Marxists would "spontaneously" interrupt the Mass by yelling or throwing things into the church. (Another great and very common tactic was to schedule a youth "dance" in front of the church and blast away with high-powered music during Mass, even if no one came to the dance.) But as things improved we began to keep all the doors wide open. This turned out to be perceived as a sign of welcome and was a great attraction.

When I looked out over the people from the altar at Mass, I could also see the people walking past outside. It was quite common to see people slow down as they passed, stretching their heads to see and hear what was going on inside. Sometimes they would stop, torn by the desire to go in or not. The prayer and music was like a magnet, drawing souls back.

Some of the faithful would hang out at the back of church, to sort of make sure that these drop-ins would feel welcome. This brought up a problem for a while. The "Pastora" Church had been traditionally the Church of the poor in Santa Clara. For a time it was the only Church to welcome black slaves. And in my time it still had the reputation of being a Church where you could go even if your clothes and shoes were on the worn side. In some parishes the desire to dress up nicely for Mass had begun to cause a problem in that those with dollars could have nice clothes and those who didn't were embarrassed by their poorer attire at Mass. So we were quite explicit in urging the people not to use the Mass as a place to show off their new dress, and NEVER in any way to give the impression of looking down on anyone for what they wore at Mass. But with the growth of foreign tourism in Cuba, prostitution, which had almost disappeared under the revolution, exploded as never before. The buying power of the dollar was so great that a prostitute could earn more in a night than a brain surgeon could in a month. So the temptation to sell one's body to the tourists was great. And the prostitutes tended to dress in such a way as to make their profession clear from a block away. So when they began stopping in at Mass, some of the older parishioners wanted to tell them that they should not enter church dressed that way. But the parish council soon made it clear to all that EVERYONE must be welcomed with courtesy and respect, regardless of how they were dressed.

I look back now with great pleasure at the Masses I celebrated in Cuba. It was a real community, trying to recover from very hard times. It was a growing community, trying to find its way. It was a welcoming community.

When I hear people complain up here in the States because their church is not air conditioned, or the music is not to their taste, or that none of the many Sunday Masses is at a really convenient time for their busy schedule, I have to bite my tongue. People who have almost lost the Mass completely tend perhaps to appreciate it more.

Before I leave this chapter on the Mass, I ought to mention one other thing. Occasionally people in Cuba would tell me that they did not go to Mass, but did listen to the Spanish Mass broadcast by "Radio Martí" from Florida. "Radio Martí" is the U.S. government radio station that constantly broadcasts exclusively to Cuba. They provide some good information not available over Cuban stations, but their purpose is to do everything possible to bring down the Communist government. So, you will hear on that station everything bad that the Communists do. You will never hear anything good that the Communists do. I doubt they would admit publicly that Castro has good teeth. In any case I thought it strange that with all the insistence on separation of Church and State the U.S. taxpayers (Catholic, Protestant, Jewish, Muslim, etc.) are paying to broadcast the Mass to Cuba, even though the Catholic churches in Cuba are open and booming. Might there perchance be a bit of utilization of religion for political purposes by the U.S. government? Strange, isn't it, that the U.S. government radio does not broadcast Christian services to Saudi Arabia where being baptized is punishable by death.

5

Other Sacraments and Ministries

HAVING SAID SOMETHING about what the Mass was like in my parishes in
Cuba, it might be helpful to say something about the other Sacraments
and Parish ministries.

BAPTISM: During the harsher years of anti-religious pressure, the practice
of baptism of infants became less common. Some people were afraid that
if they baptized their babies, they would be "marked" as non-supporters
of the revolution. The baptisms that were celebrated tended to be on the
quiet side. Some families requested private, closed-door baptisms. In other
cases there was a deep split between husband and wife, or between the
parents and grandparents, with someone totally opposed to baptism and
someone else in the same family very anxious to have the baby baptized.
Each situation had to be handled delicately, but I was told of instances
where the baby was baptized but some family members never learned of
the fact.

By the time I got there most people felt free to request baptism for
their baby without much fear. Again, police and army officers would be
more fearful of reprisals in their careers.

Those who requested baptism for their infants came from a wide range
of levels of belief. Some were fully committed to Christ and the Church.

Others had a more vague desire to do *something* spiritual for their baby. Some really didn't believe much, but wanted to baptize the infant in order to keep the grandmother happy.

Our requirements in the parish were quite small: parents had to sign up ahead of time, and the parents and God-parents had to attend a one-hour talk about the Sacrament of Baptism the week before the ceremony. There is not a great deal that can be done in one hour, but I would try to talk a bit about what baptism was, and even more about the need for educating the child in the faith and giving a good example as the child grew. I found that almost all the parents and God-parents listened with great attention. For some, it was the first serious explanation of the faith that they had ever heard. More than a few who had not been attending Mass previously started to do so afterward. It had gotten them thinking about the spirit.

The baptisms were simple and reverent celebrations. We did close all the doors of the church once the families had arrived, knowing that a few of the participants would still be nervous or afraid of being seen in Church.

For older children who had not been baptized as infants we had, of course, a year or two of weekly religious instruction with the other kids. They had to know enough of the faith, and really want to be baptized, as well as having the support of their parents. They would be baptized in groups, and it was always a very beautiful and joyous celebration.

Occasionally I would encounter parents who wanted to baptize several children right away, with no instruction at all. Sometimes they were parents who had finally gotten a U.S. visa to move to Florida, and felt ashamed to show up there with all their kids unbaptized as it might show that they had "given in" to Communism. In other cases the rumor had spread that you were more likely to get a visa from the U.S. government if you could prove that you were good church-members. But we always insisted on a full year at least of instruction for older children and adults.

The greatest joy for me was the groups of young adults who requested instruction for baptism, many of them University students. They had been subjected to years and years of Marxist indoctrination, yet grace led them to turn to Christ. They took their instructions very seriously and very joyfully, and their group baptism celebrations, usually during the Easter vigil, were marvelous. I admired them greatly. Even though religious toleration had improved, many of them had reason to believe that their baptism would hurt their chances of further education or a good job. Some of their teachers or supervisors would call them aside and urge them, for their own sake, to keep their new religious faith a secret. (We did offer them the option of being baptized in secret if they wished, but no one requested that while I was there.) We also had the joy of baptizing some medical students from Africa. They had come on scholarships to learn to be doctors, but also discovered Jesus in Cuba (which was not what the government had in mind.) Some were quite active in trying to share their new faith with the other students.

Finally, there were occasionally those who had been sent to request baptism by their Babalao (spiritual leader), as a necessary pre-condition to receive special rites in the Afro-Cuban religions. Sometimes they didn't come back once they were told that there would be a year or two of Christian instruction. Others stayed, and learned a lot.

The renewed interest in baptism was another sign of the general resurgence in things of the spirit in Cuba. I remember once talking with one of our Capuchin missionaries serving in Japan, where converts are few. When I told him about my several times being stopped on the street in Cuba by strangers who asked me how they could be sign up for baptism, he could hardly imagine it.

CONFIRMATION: The visits by Bishop Prego to administer the Sacrament of Confirmation were also very joyous occasions. Some of the candidates were teens who had been baptized as infants or young children and were now, after further instruction, freely choosing to *confirm* their faith. I admired their guts and their determination. We also had adults in the groups. While the normal Catholic practice for adults is to celebrate the Sacraments of Baptism, Confirmation, and First Communion at one ceremony, the Cuban Bishops preferred to separate the celebrations by a year to further deepen the instruction process. I had enormous admiration for Bishop Prego of Santa Clara and for all the Cuban Bishops. They had persevered through many very hard years. Bishop Prego used to tell us of his pastoral visits during the harsh years, when only two or three might have dared to prepare for confirmation in an almost empty church. The dedicated Cuban bishops and priests were now seeing the fruits of their years of persevering labor.

MATRIMONY: To discourage church weddings the Communist authorities had followed the policy of celebrating the civil marriage ceremony with much pomp and splendor. The State "Wedding Palace" was fixed up beautifully. The State provided the gown for the bride and a suit for the groom, and also the cake, beer and soda for the party. All the bells and whistles, to make the civil ceremony as majestic as a church ceremony. And to get married in church afterward would "mark" the couple as counter-revolutionary, with all the negative consequences involved. So, church weddings had become rare. In my time they were coming back. Many couples, civilly married for years or decades, now wanted the Sacrament of Matrimony. Sometimes they celebrated individually, but the Bishop would also preside at group weddings in the cathedral for a large number of couples. But there were more and more couples that wanted to start out their married life with the Sacrament. Legally, of course, they had to go through a civil ceremony first, and then have the church wedding. As with baptisms, some couples would wed behind closed doors with only a few relatives and friends who had slipped in beforehand. But there were some couples unafraid (and proud) enough to be more public and have the church doors open. I remember one couple (both were volunteer religion teachers) who decided to actually line up the wedding party outside on the church steps and march in with music. This was dangerously close to being a procession, which would be illegal, but they took the chance. People on the street were bug-eyed. Many had never seen such a thing. I remember one passerby commenting to another, "I didn't know that you could get married in a *church*!!"

The parish also had a very active Marriage Group: 20 or 25 couples who would meet once a month for a religious talk and a modest snack. They also took charge of giving the pre-marriage instructions to younger couples. It was very important for believers to support and help each other.

<u>FUNERALS</u>: During my four years in Cuba I never celebrated a funeral in church. The funeral homes, like everything else, were State institutions. Everyone had the right to a decent funeral, provided by the State, with a standard coffin for everyone. I rather liked that, having seen poor families in Central America sometimes go hopelessly into debt to pay for a funeral. But of course bringing the body to a church before burial had no place in the State funeral plans. Most people under 40 had never seen a church funeral. The kids didn't even know such a thing existed.

While I was there, however, some believing families would take a chance and invite me to go to the State funeral home and pray for their deceased loved one there. I always accepted the invitation, and we would have some prayer and scripture readings. We did it discreetly, but not secretly, and the funeral directors never caused a problem. But I would never go unless invited, even if I knew the family was practicing the faith. It was a public place, and not all believers were willing to have their faith made *that* public.

(For the same reason when I would walk down the street I would take care to never greet anyone I knew from church. If they greeted me first, fine, I would respond. But you never knew whether the person was ready to take the risk of being publicly identified as a believer by talking to the priest on the street. Maybe his boss was nearby, or maybe a cop. So I always let them make the first move. Many, indeed, would greet me warmly. Others would pretend they had not seen me, or just give an almost inperceptible nod. The adults, that is. The kids were growing up with much less fear, and the church kids would greet me warmly on the street.)

One of the great challenges to Marxism is its silence in the face of death. They may speak glowingly of revolutionary heroes "living forever in the memory of the People", but what happens after death is an emptiness for them. I recall talking once with a young doctor who came into church one day, a dedicated scientific Marxist, well educated as an atheist. But his little daughter whom he loved with all his heart had been tragically killed in a stupid accident. Scientifically speaking, a very well evolved bunch of molecules had dissolved into its component parts once again. But how could he believe that wonderful child no longer existed in any way? He had no answer at all, but when some older relative told him that they used to light candles for the dead in church he came, perhaps for the first time in his life, hoping for *something*. State funerals take care of the body well, but more and more Cubans are aware of what is lacking: the spirit.

ANNOINTING OF THE SICK: There was a fine group in the parishes that would regularly visit the sick in their homes to pray with them and bring them communion. I would accompany them regularly to administer the sacrament of the Annointing of the Sick to them as well.

Hospitals were another story. For many years, priests were not allowed to visit hospitals, except to visit a relative. "Pastoral Care" had no place in the hospital system. But by my time there most hospitals would look the other way if the family wanted to bring in a priest to visit a patient.

Again, I would never visit anyone in the hospital unless asked, lest I blow the cover of a believer who wished still to remain unknown to the authorities. And usually when a visit was requested I would ask a family member to met me outside and walk me through with them. Sometimes I would try it alone, usually with success. If the person in charge at the door was a believer: no problem. Some non-believers were also respectful of the patient's wishes. A dedicated Marxist receptionist might present problems. I was only stopped from entering a hospital once, and even that time they had an excuse since I had negligently left my identification card at home and they quoted the rule that all visitors must have I.D. Once inside it was not uncommon for people to see the priest visiting one patient who had requested a visit, and walk up and ask that their sick relative be visited also. This had to be done with care. If the staff saw you visiting several patients, there might be trouble.

PRISON MINISTRY: The operative theory had been that prisoners would be rehabilitated by firm punishment and a large dose of Marxist re-education. Since religion was judged to be harmful to everyone, priests were not allowed access to the prisons at all.

By my time, this had been changing. Prison administrators faced the fact that religion can have a good effect of changing a prisoner's anti-social conduct. "If it works, why not?" But access was limited. In my Diocese only one priest had State permission to visit the several prisons in the area (while also serving as a full-time pastor.) Generally, he got cooperation from the correction officers and could meet with prisoners who wished to do so, and even prepare for and administer baptism to those who wished, and distribute some Scripture and religious literature. He always told us, however, that most of the sharing of the faith was done by one prisoner to another.

After his visits he would give each parish the names of the prisoners from the parish territory. We had a group of dedicated volunteers, many of them ex-prisoners. With the help of the Bishop we were able to put together each month a small package of food (powdered milk, crackers, etc) and perhaps a small gift (a pencil, envelopes and writing paper, etc.) for each prisoner. We could not visit the prison, but the volunteers would visit each family, and give them the package to give to the prisoner on their next visit. We gave the packages for each prisoner, regardless of religious belief and regardless of the crime alleged to have been committed. Many non-believing families of prisoners were touched by this gesture.

While the government officials tolerated this activity (and the prison authorities were glad to see some extra food come in, as prisoners' rations were deficient) they were also often enraged by it. That was because we made no distinction between "common" criminals and political prisoners. The State was opposed to anything resembling support for (or even recognition of the existence of) political prisoners. Likewise once a month we would include special prayers for *all* prisoners from the parish at Mass, reading out their names. Some families of the prisoners would come to this Mass, and also some dissident political activists. Since we prayed publicly for the political prisoners (along with the cattle-rustlers), the government saw it as subversive. Yet they couldn't quite act against it, as we were spiritually and physically helping *all* the prisoners. This would come to a head each year at the Feast of Nuestra Señora de la Merced ("Our Lady of Mercy"). While having its historical roots in the efforts to set free Christian slaves or captives held by the Muslims during the centuries of Christian-Muslim wars, it has come (at least in Cuba) to be a special time to pray for *all* prisoners and to reach out to their families. Plain-clothes police presence is often strong at those Masses each year in September, as it is known that the names of prisoners will be read in the prayers of petition, and many supporters and family members of the prisoners will be present. Sometimes dissident leaders are detained by the police before they can reach the Church.

SACRAMENT OF RECONCILIATION: A couple of times a week I provided a scheduled time for those who wished to go to confession, and sometimes individuals would come to the parish office to request this sacrament on their own. I always found it a moving experience when people would return to church and come to confession after having abandoned their faith for many years, perhaps even publicly denying belief in God. Often they were very surprised that forgiveness and a "welcome home!" were so readily offered to them. The joy that Jesus described when the shepherd finally brings home the lost sheep is a very strong reality in Cuba.

At the same time, I always had to be aware of the possibility that the "penitent" might actually be a police agent sent there to set a trap, or to see what advice I might give to someone confessing something that the State would be very interested in knowing about. More than once a parish member would take me aside in private to warn me that this or that person (seemingly very sincere) was actually a spy sent to infiltrate the church as deeply as possible. They could be very convincing. Even the Seminary had to be very careful to try to weed out potential "vocations" who might actually be well prepared "moles" from the State Security. Likewise I took prudent precautions to try to make sure that the place of Confession was not bugged by the State. We enjoyed a greater degree of religious freedom than had been the case in earlier years, but you had to keep in mind always that it was a police State where the right of privacy was not recognized.

6

Human Rights

WHILE I HAVE spoken already about the improved (but still deficient) respect for religious rights in Cuba, talking about our modest efforts in support of prisoners leads me naturally to say something about other human rights.

It should be noted that the rights of freedom of speech, press, association, travel, peaceful assembly, due process of law, fair trial, voting and political action continue to be severely limited. The argument presented by the Cuban government is that because the Communist Party is *the* Party of the People, any other political party must, by definition, be against the interests of the people. And they claim that because it is the Communist Party that defends the sovereignty of Cuba, any other political party or group must, likewise, be guilty of treasonous collaboration with Cuba's enemies. And so on down the line: *only* the Communist labor unions, professional associations, sports clubs, newspapers, radio and TV stations, etc., etc., etc. serve the people. Any independent group is seen as a dangerous threat.

The laws that back up this ideology are broad. Any criticism can be treated as treason. Even speaking the truth about problems in the economy can be classified as "collaboration with enemy propaganda". And once the accusation is made, the victim has little chance of a real defense or even of legal counsel in the Cuban courts. The harshness of the penalties can vary. Sometimes the government lets people get away with a little bit for a time, then it suddenly cracks down harshly.

When faced with the question of what I, as an American pastor of two Cuban parishes could do to defend these rights I had to recognize two things. First, that as a foreigner my residence visa could be cancelled by the Cuban government at any time if I in any way annoyed them. So the question was always "Should I stay and do what I can to help, or try to do more and get kicked out immediately? Would my people be better off having a priest with them even though his hands were tied in many areas, or to be without a priest because he took a stronger public stance and got booted out?" And I was not only a foreigner, but an American as well. So any activity in favor of human rights would have, for the Communists, the flavor of American imperialism. And anyone connected with me could be seen, automatically, as a treasonous collaborator.

Second, a priest or Bishop, (whether Cuban or foreign) had also to ask himself: "Is what I might possibly hope to accomplish by speaking up more forcefully for human rights worth the reprisals that my people would suffer because of my actions?" I know that there are sincere and dedicated people who believe that the Church in Cuba has not done and is not doing enough to defend human rights. Usually they are not the people who would suffer the reprisals. My parish members, the ones who come to Mass, take part in parish organizations and send their kids to religious instruction, were usually not in favor of our taking a heroic but futile public stance in favor of human rights, because they knew it could mean the loss of their church, their leaders, their ability to share the faith with their children, and the limited religious freedom that they had at long last obtained. I believe (I hope I am mistaken) that some of the more outspoken people in Washington and Miami who demand that the Cuban Church be more drastic in defense of human rights, really hope that it *would* provoke a violent reaction from the Cuban government, because it serves their purpose to make the Communists look as bad as possible, no matter who gets hurt.

Given these challenges, what went on in my parishes regarding human rights? I think we did what we could. Cuba was one of the signatories (and in fact, one of the major authors) of the "United Nations Universal Declaration of Human Rights" and has never taken back that approval. So, at the parish members' request, I managed to photocopy a modest amount of copies of that declaration (with no commentary whatsoever). We made copies available for a token price to anyone who wanted to read it, and we had parish study sessions on it. It was obvious which rights the Government recognized (food, health, employment) and which it suppressed (speech, press, assembly). The Communists did not like the fact that we did this, but could not quite act against us since Cuba officially recognized the document.

(I did, however, turn down the offer of outsiders to provide us with unlimited copies. We studied only our blurry "made in Cuba" copies.)

We also helped make available copies of the Cuban laws concerning the rights of prisoners and of the accused, so that at least some feeble legal challenge could be raised when the authorities violated even their own laws.

I also tried to present the truth to outside observers. I would speak freely to any visiting journalist or visitor that dropped in, describing truthfully and without exaggeration what was good and what was bad. I usually met them in the front office with the doors and wide windows completely open so that anyone passing by could see who I was with and hear what we were saying. This, of course, sometimes enraged the authorities as they wish only good news to come out of Cuba. I several times invited the Communist officials to join us as well to give their point of view, but they never accepted.

I recall that in summer of 1997 the remains of Che Guevara, the great Argentine hero of the Revolution in Cuba were finally exhumed in Bolivia and returned to Cuba, along with those of several companions. He had been executed there without trial after his capture. (The U.S. government was deeply involved in his capture and execution.) Che had been trying to start the revolution violently there as well. The remains were received with tremendous solemnity over several days, and brought in triumphal procession all the way from Havana to Santa Clara, (where I was), to be re-buried in the huge monument and plaza which had been built there in his honor years before. Every solemn act and speech was televised, and a number of foreign reporters showed up to cover the celebration. But in Santa Clara a small group of Cuban human rights activists decided to hold a modest activity in support of several of their relatives and friends who were in prison. About 10 or 20 gathered quietly in a home, with a Cuban flag, and simply held a quiet fast. They hoped that the foreign journalists might listen to and publish their stories. But the Communists were terrified of such a "public" protest. The house was raided before the reporters arrived, all were arrested and many received harsh prison sentences for such a "counter-revolutionary" act. What I did to support them was simply to tell visiting reporters what had happened, and to tell them where they could find other family members who were willing to take the risk and publicly talk to them "on the record". Later when I was told of political prisoners who had begun a "fast to the death" in prison I likewise tried to make sure that the foreign press knew about it, so that the Government would be obliged to try to keep them alive, knowing that the outside world was watching.

Other parish activities had a more indirect influence. When I reorganized the Pastoral Council (Catholic Canon Law recommends that every parish have a group of lay people forming a Pastoral Council) I asked each organized group in the parish to elect one representative. So, the choir members elected one of theirs, the children's catechists another, and so on for the adult catechists, youth group, marriage group, prison committee, etc.

They were quite astonished and delighted. Each group would meet and share suggestions as to who their representative should be. Then they would vote by each member secretly writing a name on a slip of paper. The votes were counted in the presence of all. If no one got a majority, the vote would be repeated between the two who had gotten the most votes. I recall one middle-aged lady, a visitor of the sick, saying afterwards "It's the first time I have ever voted!" Actually she had "voted" many times in the past in local elections. Voting is not mandatory, but strongly encouraged. The lists are checked, and if you haven't shown up to vote by the late afternoon, "volunteers" may visit your home to see if you are sick and offer to bring you a ballot. So the turn-out is 98% or so. But usually there is only one candidate to vote for in each category. If there are two candidates, as now happens sometimes, both are of the same Communist party, and all candidates are cleared from above. You may, if you wish, spoil the ballot in the secrecy of the voting booth, and some do. But you have no real choice of candidates. So our Parish Pastoral Council elections were quite a revolutionary experience. I also empowered the Finance Council of the parish. I never saw the collections. They would collect and count it, spend it for what was needed and give me a report at the end of the month. I tried to emphasize that it was *their* Parish and I was working for *them*.

Another way that the Church in Cuba defends human rights is by using its very limited capacity to print and distribute materials. In recent years the Communists have allowed Bishops, and sometimes even parishes, to buy photocopy machines, paper, ink, toner, etc. and there are some small-scale diocesan and parish publications. While direct criticism of human rights abuses are rare and weak in these publications (remembering that the State can seize such equipment at any time, or simply sell no more paper to the Church) they offer an important service by providing at least some independent commentary and criticism. On of the greatest services is to make available sections of the Pope's own strong commentaries on human rights, and the documents of the Second Vatican Council, the Latin American Bishops' official statements, and the official statements of the Cuban Bishops individually and collectively. When the authorities complain about such statements, one can honestly respond "Well, *I* didn't say that, **The Pope** said that. Send **Him** your complaint if you don't agree." (As we will see later, the Pope's televised talks during his visit to Cuba contain pages of stuff that any Cuban could be arrested for saying out loud. But since the government let *him* say that in Cuba, his words can be reprinted and distributed.)

In my parish we had managed to obtain after some years a small portable electronic typewriter which had the capacity of printing in several sizes and styles of type. We had also a small desk-top insert-one-blank-page-at-a-time photocopier and enough paper and toner to run off a few things. How we got these things would be worth a chapter in itself, but it's a story that ought not be told now. Anyway one of the parish members, Angel Cristobal (I can mention his name since he and his wife and child have left Cuba) would work hard every month to carefully type up a one-page (8½x11, both sides) Parish Bulletin with a mixture of teachings, news, quotes from official Church documents and aspects of the religious history of Cuba that were no longer taught in schools. He would carefully choose the smallest type-size that people could read, and fill both sides of the sheet edge to edge, yet break things into columns and boxes and even include line drawings so that it was an attractive and readable little bulletin. We stuffed more things into that page each month than you would think possible. Then we would send the copy to the Bishop to examine and correct. Bishop Prego (now deceased; may God reward him for a lifetime of heroic service to the Cuban Church) always had the final say as to what was printed or not printed in it. Once he gave us the final version we would run off 150 or 200 copies one at a time (had to stop the little machine every 10 copies to cool it off). We would sell them for a token price in the back of Church, and they circulated widely. It was probably one of the best "newspapers" in Cuba, which says a lot about the competition. The Communist authorities would regularly call in the Bishop to complain about the content, and he would stand up to them for the truth (and let them know quite clearly that *He* was responsible for every word printed, to keep the heat off us.) His own (larger) Diocesan print-outs, as well as those of other Dioceses, were also well-read and much appreciated by believers and non-believers alike.

Once again, the government's best response to human rights criticism was to ignore the criticisms and go on the attack. If anyone pointed the flaws in Cuban elections they could say "And just what percentage of citizens actually *votes* in the famous American 'democratic' elections?" (And they knew the miserable percentages by heart). Point out the lack of choice in candidates and they would point out that every Cuban Communist candidate was an honest factory or farm worker, and then run through the statistics of how many millions of dollars in campaign contributions it takes to get elected in the U.S., and what the odds are of a non-millionaire getting into the U.S. Senate. They would also have older Cubans relate how the "free" elections in Cuba used to be before the revolution, with the frauds and vote-buying, and the benevolence of the U.S. government toward any Cuban dictator who followed U.S. orders.

Another very effective method that the Communists used frequently when U.S. leaders would demand democratic reforms in Cuba was to simply and accurately point out our hypocrisy. Our government had no qualms about participating very actively in the overthrow of democratically elected governments in Guatemala and Chile, and in cooperating most cordially with the military dictators that replaced them (as long as they went along with U.S. policy). And there is no sign of the U.S. demanding that Saudi Arabia hold democratic elections or grant religious freedom, and certainly no threat of a U.S. trade embargo against *them*. Yet this is what we do regarding Cuba. The rest of the world laughs at us. Every year the United Nations votes overwhelmingly to demand that the U.S. lift its economic embargo against Cuba. Last time, if I remember right, only Israel and Uzbekistan voted with the United States. Our inconsistency in demanding reforms in Cuba that we do not demand elsewhere makes it much easier for Cuba to deflect the justifiable criticisms of its human rights record.

And of course, the Communists also had plenty of ammunition to use against the Church when we said anything about human rights. The Catholic Church's defense of human rights is a rather recent (and blessed) development. You don't have to go far back to find Popes condemning freedom of the press, saying that only the "truth" has the right to be expressed. When Pope John Paul II arrived in Cuba in 1998 Castro knew that he was going to bring up the question of human rights in his talks, as he does wherever he visits. So he tried to beat the Pope to the punch in his welcoming remarks at the airport by going on at some length about the abuses committed by the Spanish Catholic Conquistadores against the native residents of Cuba. And the Communists ask where the Church leadership was when it was the Batista regime, and not the Communists, who were committing human rights abuses. Now, thanks be to God, our Church has a much better and more consistent teaching in defense of human rights, but our track record over the centuries has not been too good.

So, my experience was that the Church was doing what was possible in defense of human rights in Cuba. I'll listen with respect to those who say that more should have been done. But in the back of my mind I'll be thinking also: "*You* weren't there, under the boot. *We* were. We did what we could."

7

Health Care

ONE NICE THING about working in Cuba, especially after 20 years in Central America, was to find people in good health with excellent (free) medical care. The kids are obviously healthy and sufficiently nourished. The main complaint that I would hear very, very often was of the shortage of some medicines and medical supplies. Not that there were *no* medicines, but that the exact medicines that the specialists prescribed were often lacking or in short supply.

One of the basic principles of Castro's regime is that every Cuban has the right to complete, excellent and free medical care throughout life. And he can (and very often does) justifiably boast of what has been accomplished toward that goal. Cuba has trained so many doctors that the ratio of doctors to population is probably the highest in the world, and medical students come from other countries to study there. The infant mortality rate is about on a par with that of the United States, and far better than that of the Latino or black population in the United States. On average a Cuban child has a better chance of reaching adulthood in Cuba than does a Latino or black child in the U.S. The percentage of children in Cuba who have been vaccinated against childhood diseases is likewise among the highest in the world. And while Cuba cannot produce all the types or quantities of medicines that it needs, its pharmaceutical industry has developed several respected drugs that are sold internationally (even though the U.S. will not buy them). There are an abundance of hospitals and health clinics, and each family is assigned to a neighborhood family doctor for primary care. Special residential clinics are provided for women with problem pregnancies.

But maintaining such a universal free system is very expensive. During the years when the former Soviet Union poured in substantial subsidies, the health program grew and thrived. With the collapse of the U.S.S.R. and the cut-off of all that aid, the Cuban health care system has deteriorated. The number of medicines available, and the quantities available, have dropped markedly. Even aspirin availability is limited. While trying to produce more, Cuba has also tried to develop alternative (and less expensive) treatments. Herbal remedies (carefully prepared) are available in the State drug stores. Spas offering treatments with natural hot springs and mud are promoted. Even such things as magnetism are being promoted as new treatments. But the shortages of all things persist. Even in the hospitals, patients are now urged to bring their own sheets, and cannot count on having soap or toilet paper provided by the hospital. Families are urged to provide a relative or friend to be a "companion" for the patient, and the staff is not shy about inviting visitors to help mop the floors and feed the patients. A highly trained and competent surgeon may find himself or herself having to cancel pending surgeries because the supply of rubber gloves has run out.

Along with these deficiencies, however, the government also promotes "medical tourism". Sick people (with money) from other countries come to Cuba for operations or treatments provided either in special "foreigner-only, dollar-only, pay-up-front-in-cash only" hospitals, or in special wings of the general hospitals, all much better equipped and staffed than the "people's" hospitals. Some come because the operations are cheaper than in their home countries, others come in desperation to try treatments or surgeries offered by Cuban doctors which are not accepted in other countries (such as experimental treatments for Parkinson's disease.). It causes great resentment among the Cuban people to see foreigners getting better treatment than they do. But the government argues that the dollars brought in this way are used to buy the foreign medicines that are needed and that are then given free to the Cubans. (Cubans who work in the tourist industry are likewise strongly encouraged to voluntarily give part of their hard-currency tips to the State to buy needed cancer medicines abroad.)

The Cuban government, of course, tends to place the blame for all medical shortages on the U.S. embargo laws (always referred to as the "criminal blockade"). Although exaggerated there is some truth contained in the charge. Although in theory U.S. companies can get a Treasury Department permit to sell their medicines and equipment in Cuba, in practice the red tape created by the U.S. makes it extremely difficult. Private or religious medical assistance groups in the States likewise have to get such permits to donate free medicine, and have greater success than the companies (although the U.S. would much prefer that the Churches try to have their own health system, to "show up" the Communists.) So some medicines that could have been bought from the U.S. directly must be brought in from other countries at greater expense. This provides the Communists with an excellent propaganda weapon. While I was there, for example, the Austrian company which had been selling heart pacemakers to the Cuban health care system was bought up by a larger international company based in the U.S. So the Austrian company sent a letter explaining that since they were now a "U.S." company, U.S. law now prohibited them from selling the pacemakers to Cuba. Cuba would have to find them elsewhere, while the patients were told to wait. It was headline news in Cuba.

It can be questioned, however, whether such shortages would disappear if the U.S. allowed free trade. A country has to be pretty productive to pay for universal free health care, and the Communist system tends not to be efficiently productive. But I find that most Americans are not even aware that the U.S. government sometimes uses the restriction of medicines as a political tool. And those Americans who become aware don't like it. We are, I think, generally a compassionate people, and we exclude the sick and wounded as targets even in war. But our government does not always express the goodness of our people. I remember when I was serving in a rural parish in Nicaragua in 1988. It was a huge territory, and we traveled long distances by mule or boat to try to visit the many scattered rural communities. At that time the U.S. was financing, training and arming the "Contras" who were trying to overthrow the Sandinista government in Nicaragua because it was considered too leftist. My parish, in Rama on the east side of the country, was split. The government controlled parts, and the "Contras" controlled other parts. The Sandinista government was trying to imitate the Cuban model of free universal health care, and had a nation-wide program of vaccination against measles. But I would visit village after village in the "Contra" controlled area and the people would tell me how many children had died of measles. The "Contras" (the so-called "freedom fighters" the U.S. taxpayers were paying) refused to let the government vaccination teams enter their areas, knowing that the people would become grateful to the government for the free health care. I doubt you could find one American in a hundred who would approve of "our side" letting kids die of measles in the name of anti-communism. Likewise, I didn't hear of any protest in the U.S. when "our" Contras were filmed by reporters using Red Cross helicopters to deliver arms and soldiers. When I was serving in El Salvador I saw the same thing: heavily armed government troops (armed and paid by the U.S.) using a Red Cross vehicle as military transport. So, we as a nation have given the Communists something to base their denunciations on.

The American Catholic Church has been successfully delivering large quantities of medical assistance to Cuba, with permits from the U.S. Treasury Department. Almost all is delivered to the Cuban government health system, as that is the most effective way of getting it to the people. Most Cubans who receive this help are not even aware that it came from the American Catholic Church. In this I think that the U.S. Church is following very well the teachings of Jesus: to practice charity toward the sick because they are sick, not in order to "win them over" or to make the Communists look bad. I was often told that many officials in Cuba have been very favorably impressed by that generosity. The Catholic Church of Germany gave a wonderful example of charitable medical aid. Instead of donating German medicines (on which German companies would make a profit) they donated chemicals and raw materials to the Cuban pharmaceutical plants so that they could make their *own* medicines. "Give a person a fish and he eats for a day, teach him to fish and he eats for a lifetime."

While some of the medicine provided by foreign Churches is (with Cuban government permission) made available directly to the Church in Cuba for distribution, the Church is not allowed to have its own clinics or health care system. So, some parishes (with government tolerance) distribute some medicine right from the parish offices. Because of the extensive medical care system in Cuba the people who come to the churches looking for help are not looking for a doctor. They have already seen their primary care physician, then often been referred to a specialist. Their sickness has been correctly diagnosed, and the proper prescription(s) given. But often the doctors have to tell them: "This is the medicine you need, but we don't have any right now. If you can get some from relatives overseas, or find a church that is giving it away, great. Otherwise we'll have to use something else that we have, even if it won't be as effective." If the patient does not have overseas relatives who can send the medicine, he or she has to troop from church to church to church to beg, hoping to find some.

I did not care for that system, so I would not do any distribution of medicine from my parishes. Sometimes I would receive modest shipments of medicine or medical supplies from other countries. (People who would send me medicine from the States, since they did not have a Treasury Department license, would send it to someone in Canada or elsewhere, where a friend would re-mail it to me in Cuba.) I would either give it directly to the hospital, or to doctors I knew and trusted so they could give it directly to their patients as needed. I figured that to be the most effective way of getting it to those who needed it.

A couple of times when I had some dollars available I would ask the doctors in the parish what they needed most. Often they asked for books instead of medicines. The economic problems have caused the medical libraries to cancel subscriptions to foreign medical journals, and to postpone buying new editions of medical reference texts. So sometimes the docs would give me the name of a particular medical encyclopedia or professional text and I was able to order them from Spain for them. They would read them voraciously to catch up on the latest improvements and discoveries in medicine, and share the texts with the other docs.

The Communist authorities fear that the churches would use medical care as a tool to win new converts, so do not wish to see the churches running a competitive health care program. They have a point. The churches which have medicines (usually in quite limited quantities) are supposed to give it out to those with prescriptions on a first-come-first-served basis, without requiring that the patient be a church member. Generally it is done like that, although in my experience it was not uncommon for churches to secretly hold back some for their favored members. People coming in off the street might be told "there is no more" while a choir member or catechist might find that there really is some more stashed away. The temptation to play favorites is great.

I was never aware of any black market in medicines. Sometimes some donated medicines from abroad would end up being sold for dollars in the government stores, but it would be defended as necessary to get the cash to buy even more urgently needed medicines abroad. But there was a problem of an informal sort of black market. When medicines became available in a hospital in limited quantities, there was always the temptation for some of the medical staff to try to take some home to keep "just in case" for emergencies in their own families. And if they managed to get a stash at home, word might get out and friends or neighbors might approach privately to beg for some. Or perhaps favors might be offered in exchange. Helping the refrigerator repair man get some needed medicine for his daughter might get your broken refrigerator fixed right away instead of after two years on the waiting list. Scarcity encourages ingenuity, and sometimes corruption.

I had my own minor challenge in that regard. For years in Central America I would come down every so often with a severe ear infection. It was very painful, and I would go deaf on one side for weeks. Since the doctors had found the right antibiotic to cure it, I would get a big prescription for it filled while visiting the U.S. and then keep it with me to be ready whenever the infection might come back, as I was often far from any pharmacies in Central America. So likewise in Cuba I had my private supply of "just in case" antibiotic. Then one day a worker doing repairs in the church came to me. He had hurt his hand days before, and it was badly infected. The doctors told him what antibiotic was needed, but at that moment there was none available. So he asked me if I might have any. I'm sorry to say that I told him no (afraid of losing my private supply). But the teachings of Jesus have a way of sinking in, so I called him back later and gave him the antibiotic. I was not very cheerful about it, since I dreaded getting hit again by my ear infection and having no medicine. It made me reflect. In Central America I had been instrumental in obtaining and giving away truckloads of medicine. Big hero! But when it came to giving away a little medicine that I might need *myself* it was quite a different story.

Anyway, throughout my four years in Cuba there was a steady stream of people coming to seek medicine at the church office, and I could tell them honestly that I had already given what I had received to the doctors or hospitals.

I perhaps ought to mention as an aside that while in Cuba I had to have a hernia operation. A doctor who was a very faithful parish member assured me that they could do a good job there, so I had it done in the local hospital. (Since I was a permanent resident, I got the same medical care as the rest of the Cubans.) It went fine, and has given me no trouble in the years since then. I did however ask a foreigner who was coming to visit me in Cuba a week before the surgery to buy as many packs of disposable surgical gloves as he could squeeze into spaces in his suitcase.

So, I was able to give the surgeons not only gloves for my surgery, but enough for several dozen other operations as well.

Most of my parish members in Cuba were by that time quite used to having excellent free medical care, so they often complained bitterly about the shortages. When I told them that in many "democratic" countries in Latin America medical care was much worse than in Cuba, they could not really believe it. And those Cubans who moved to Florida were often in shock to find that they had to pay a doctor hundreds of dollars for an office visit and tests, and that the first question asked on entering a hospital was sometimes not "how sick are you?" but "do you have insurance?"

In Cuba, any mention of shortages or deficiencies in the State medical services is greatly frowned upon by the government, and sometimes suppressed as "cooperation with enemy propaganda" (unless the shortage is clearly and totally blamed on the United States). On the other hand I have more than once been denounced in the States for pointing out the facts of what the Cuban medical system has accomplished and is accomplishing. To admit those facts is considered "supporting communism" or "supporting Castro". Often neither extreme wants to hear the truth.

Again, I saw the reality of the Cuban health care system through the lens of my previous 20 years in Central America. So I greatly admired Cuba for providing its people with a health care system that most Central Americans would not even dream of. I did not like watching children die for lack of basic medical care in Central America when often much of even what little money should have been available for medical care was stolen by those in power. The Cuban Communists have done some great things as far as medical care is concerned, and they deserve credit for it.

8

TV and Radio

I THINK YOU can learn something about a country by observing what they have on TV and radio (which makes me rather depressed about our own future when I scan the channels here in the U.S.) I'm not an expert on the subject, but I'll try to share what I saw in Cuba, and what I think it meant.

There were only two channels available, both (of course) government stations. They usually broadcasted only from around 5 p.m. until 11 or 11:30 or so. The one exception was Sunday mornings when they would show cartoons and kids' shows. More than one parish member thought that this was done in order to give the kids an attractive alternative to going to Church on Sunday.

The news shows were well done professionally, but contained only what the Communists wanted announced. Good news was the norm. Negative news about the Cuban situation was almost unknown. Any hint of criticism of anything the government did was nonexistent. Reports on the progress of the sugar planting, harvest and processing were constant, never mentioning the constantly falling actual production. Crimes were generally reported only if they had been solved and the criminals arrested. I never noticed them giving any reports that were untrue. They just left out any unfavorable truths and reported anything positive they could find.

Movies, mostly American, were popular, sometimes dubbed in Spanish, sometimes subtitled. The people told me that this was a more recent development, as previously the TV relied more on Russian stuff. By far the most popular shows were the "telenovelas" (soap operas), going on for dozens or hundreds of episodes. Some were Cuban made, and less popular. The huge hits were soap operas from Brazil (dubbed into Spanish from Portuguese), Venezuela or Mexico. All the twists and turns of romance, betrayal, triumph and tragedy were avidly followed night after night.

While very popular and entertaining, most of these soap operas were actually undermining the government's own propaganda efforts. The official message was that Communist Cuba was the best country in the world. But the viewers could see every night the clothes, cars, food, telephones, gadgets and lifestyle of the "corrupt" capitalist nations and compare them to their own reality. I recall once watching a U.S. movie on TV in Cuba about a struggling young boxer. (No, not "Rocky", this was one I never heard of.) Anyway, it was supposed to be a tragic story of a poor family where the husband risked his life in the ring despite health problems that might cause his death from the blows. He does it to get his family out of poverty, while his loving wife begs him to stop and just put up with their hardships. But in one scene she is trying to convince him while she serves his supper. But she slaps on his plate a slab of beef which would be more meat than a Cuban family would get from their ration card in a month! I had only been in Cuba for a while, but when I saw that steak I forgot all about the plot of the movie and just thought "Wow! What a piece of meat!" All Cuba was drooling over the "poor" family's steak instead of looking down on the brutal capitalist system.

Religion likewise slipped onto Cuban TV through some of the soap operas. There was no religious programming whatsoever in Cuba (except later for the Pope's visit), but sometimes religion was present in the plots of the soaps. Sometimes the church came out looking good, sometimes the plot made it look bad, but it was *there* as a normal part of the life of people.

I remember one enormously popular series from Brazil. Two of the characters were children: a boy and a girl, both about 8. They were the best of friends, although actually the convoluted romances of the plot showed that they were actually half-brother-and-sister and did not know it. Anyway, while their elders alternately loved, betrayed, helped and cheated each other night after night, the kids enjoyed a sweet and lovely friendship. Then the plot thickened. The boy (through the evil machinations of the chief villainess) fell gravely ill and went to the hospital. Night after night his struggle for life was the background of the rest of the plot. And night after night the little girl character would pray for her little friend before going to bed, asking God to make him better. Well, the kid got better and that crisis of the telenovela was solved. But something interesting happened. Every day there were little groups of 5 or 6 kids at a time going into the church on their way to and from school. Some were banging on the door to get in at 7 a.m. Most were not "regulars" at church. What happened? They saw the little girl on TV praying every night. Many of those kids had never seen, heard or experienced prayer so far in their lives. On seeing it, they instinctively liked it (like ducks to water) and wanted to try it. The kids who knew how to pray would proudly show their little friends how to kneel, how to make a sign of the cross, etc. The teachers were not happy when they heard about it. The soap opera had counter-acted some "invincible" atheistic indoctrination.

There were also two very popular soap operas from Japan of all places, perfectly dubbed into Spanish. But both followed the fortunes of Japanese families over several generations. They were very interesting, and very well done, and people would talk about them the next day. But both had the same message: that the introduction of full capitalism and western democracy after Japan's defeat in World War II allowed everybody to get rich by working hard! They even had a Japanese Communist character who had studied in Russia. He ended up owning a supermarket, and commented ruefully that the American conquerors had at the stroke of a pen accomplished all the land reform he had dreamed of, and that the best thing that ever happened to Japan was the American occupation! I could only assume that the Cuban leadership does not watch the soap operas that they allow to be broadcast.

Fidel, however, considers himself a true TV star. He presumes that his speeches, even if they go on for 4 hours, are the best programs possible. To play it safe, however, his speeches are on *both* channels, so there is no competition. But the speeches are never announced in advance. Suddenly the planned program does not appear, and there he is. They likewise never announce how long he will talk, or whether the soap opera or programmed movie will be shown after he is done, or postponed until the next night. So, if you are desperate to see the next chapter of the soap, you leave Fidel on, even for hours, because whenever he stops they *might* show the soap.

It doesn't have to be a big speech by Fidel to interrupt the programming. The welcoming ceremony for the new ambassador from Mongolia will likewise knock out the soaps. And sometimes instead of a 3-hour speech, Fidel will give a 3-hour press conference in which four tame reporters will take turns tossing him puff-ball questions to which he will give half-hour answers.

I must admit that I consider him a brilliant speaker, and that has, I think, helped him stay in power. I was surprised to find that I could listen to him for an hour without getting bored, even while I picked apart what he was saying and what he was leaving out. He has a gift, and uses it. But with a captive audience he goes on and on and on. When he limits himself in order to speak to an international group he can give an extraordinarily effective talk for 10 or 15 minutes.

The U.S. tries to counter the effectiveness of Cuban TV as propaganda by spending millions of dollars every year to broadcast "TV Martí" to Cuba from Florida. But Cuba easily blocks the signal, so no one in Cuba ever sees it. This, of course, does not stop us from spending more and more millions to keep on broadcasting it to no one.

The U.S. propaganda *radio* station "Radio Martí" is, however, seldom jammed and is widely listened to. They offer news, commentary and even some entertainment. They also, as I mentioned, offer some highly politicized religious programs. I enjoyed listening to "Radio Martí", and I think they provide a useful service. Unfortunately, they insist on being a propaganda tool. They do not even try to give a balanced and fair report. What is bad about the Cuban system is truthfully reported. What is good is totally ignored. Sometimes it gets rather silly. I recall one program where they were reporting complaints that due to the shortages in Cuba some hospitals were no longer offering free car service to patients to come and go to the hospital. (We're not talking about emergency ambulance service, just cars to pick up and drop off walking patients). I was thinking "Hey, *U.S.* hospitals don't offer free car service, and you're criticizing Cuban hospitals for *no longer always* providing it?" If they gave a more balanced picture they would be more effective.

Those with short-wave radios (not uncommon in Cuba, and quite legal) also tune in to many foreign stations. Sometimes you can even pick up regular Florida stations at night. TV antennas, however, are not allowed to be directed toward Florida. They must point to the nearest Cuban transmitter. With the influx of foreign tourists, however, the government has realized that the tourists want their TV. So government satellite receivers were set up, and they beamed the foreign programs to the tourist hotels. Cubans, however, are both smart and well educated in technology, so you would see home-made antennas, some made out of pie plates and scrap metal, hoisted up on poles to catch the "forbidden" tourist channels. Others would build their own satellite receivers, including unscramblers constantly updated. Sometimes the government would crack down harder on this, and sometimes just look the other way. I more than once saw home-made satellite TV unscramblers being sold on the street in Havana.

So, I found that Cubans are quite hungry for information and entertainment from outside. They manage to get a little over their own TV and radio system despite the government's efforts at control, and seek more as best they can. For myself, while I believe that everyone should have free access to information and culture, I do in fact as a pastor dread to think of what will be dumped into Cuban homes once such freedom is finally achieved. TV can build up, but it can also destroy. As a wise person once said, "Keep your mind fully open, and people will try to dump their garbage there."

9

The Exodus

WHEN I WOULD answer the door at my rectory in Cuba and find a nervous stranger there, I would guess that it was probably someone who wanted to leave Cuba and somehow thought that as an American I had some "influence" to help them out.

A common reality in the Central American countries where I had served previously was the desire of many people to go to the United States in order to earn money. From Central America this usually meant taking the long overland journey up through Mexico to cross the border there. Along the way there were risks of being exploited or even killed by both the "coyotes" who demanded pay to move the migrants through the borders and by some of the police who held absolute power over the illegals, as well as the dangers of the final trek across the deserts of the American Southwest. Those who could raise enough money might manage to fly to the U.S. as visitors and then just disappear into the workforce when their visas expired. The numbers were, and are, huge. While I served in Guatemala in 1994 it was reported, I think accurately, that at any given moment about 10% of the Guatemalan population was in the United States working.

I could understand and sympathize with their desire, but at the same time it was my mission to serve the people who stayed behind. And I lamented the loss to those countries of some of their most talented and hard-working people. So, I never tried either to encourage or to discourage their efforts to go North. It was personal decision of each one to make.

So in Cuba I likewise found that many people desired to leave, to go to the U.S. or some other country. For some the motivation was, I think, primarily economic. For others it was the desire to live and raise their families in a freer society. For most, in my opinion, it was for a mixture of both motives.

But in Cuba, unlike Mexico or Central America, the government for a long time tried to stop, by police action, the exodus. At other times, to bring pressure on the United States, the Communists would allow or even encourage, massive emigration. The Cuban government's official (and much repeated) explanation for the large number of Cubans that wanted to leave was that the U.S. embargo laws had so damaged the economy that people were forced to look elsewhere for economic reasons, and that if it weren't for the embargo everything would be great in Cuba and hardly anybody would want to leave. The anti-Castro groups in the States tend to explain it as purely the desire to escape Communism. My own impression, from dealing with people one-on-one for four years there was that the truth (as so often happens) lies between the extremes.

There is one thing that makes the situation of Cuban emigrants different from those from all other parts of the world: by special U.S. law any *Cuban* who succeeds in placing one foot on dry American sand is automatically granted permanent residency and the right to work. Illegal immigrants from *all* other countries can be deported once caught, even if they have worked here for years. (If the potential deportee claims that he or she would be persecuted for political or religious reasons in their home country, they can request asylum, but have to prove their case one by one.) So the Cuban government claims, correctly I believe, that the U.S. is *encouraging* Cubans to risk the voyage in makeshift rafts, or to highjack boats or planes, by promising them residency if they survive the trip. One can easily imagine how many rafts full of Haitians would be at sea tomorrow (and how many people would drown) if the U.S. were to declare that any Haitian who reached our shore alive could stay permanently. And if the U.S were to announce that any Mexican or Central American that managed to set foot on American soil could stay, millions would be on the march North tomorrow.

During my stay there the Cuban government decided for a time to let anyone who wanted to leave by raft to just go freely. They could build their rafts right under the eyes of the police. The resulting crisis produced an agreement between Cuba and the U.S. According to the agreement, Cuba would allow at least 20,000 people a year to emigrate legally to the U.S., and the U.S. would receive them. But anyone intercepted *at sea* by the U.S. would be returned to Cuba against their will. Cuba in turn promised that anyone forcibly returned by the U.S. would not be prosecuted or persecuted for having tried to leave. And the U.S. diplomats in Havana were granted the right to visit the returnees periodically throughout the island to see if that promise had been kept. But even with this agreement if any Cuban could illegally reach the U.S. by raft (or hired speedboat from Florida) he or she could stay. This led to the almost unbelievable scenes shown on TV of the U.S. authorities struggling in the surf with arriving Cubans, trying to stop them before they could touch dry sand. The Cubans knew that if they could just break free and take two more steps, they could stay in the States. If the U.S. cops were strong enough to hold them and put them in a boat, back to Cuba they went.

Every few weeks an American destroyer or Coast Guard cutter would sail into a selected Cuban port and turn over to the Cuban authorities all those caught at sea. The Red Cross observed the hand-over, as did the U.S. diplomats who recorded their names and addresses to guarantee their protection.

As I had done in Central America, in Cuba I neither encouraged nor discouraged emigration. That decision was theirs alone to make. So when people came to the parish office looking for help to emigrate, they found sympathy but no help from me. For one thing, I *had* no influence to get anyone a visa. And even if I did I would not have used it. But the number who requested visas to go to the States was far beyond the number to be granted each year, so people would clutch at any straw to try to get one. And they had many obstacles to overcome. First, they had to apply for one of the visas, and fulfill the U.S. requirements. Then if they were among those selected they had to fulfill the Cuban requirements. Getting a passport, producing photocopies of needed documents (where private photocopiers were almost non-existent), getting the required physical exam (which had to be paid for in dollars) and then getting enough dollars to actually buy a ticket: each step was a major headache. Unless the person had family overseas who could help financially with dollars, it was almost impossible. On top of that there were the family complications: what if the wife wants to go, but the husband doesn't? What if there are kids from a previous marriage and one biological parent does not agree? What if the parents want to go but the kids don't?

Another frequent problem had to do with the young women who wanted to get married to a visiting tourist (*fast*) so as to leave with him (and later bring out the whole family). Catholic marriage is a very serious lifetime sacramental commitment, requiring thoughtful preparation, so they left the rectory very disappointed. Sometimes the relationships were genuine. Sometimes they were arranged specifically to get out of Cuba. And sometimes it was the case of a young Cuban who had gotten involved in prostitution to earn dollars from the tourists (and get into the best restaurants, nightclubs and stores with them). Any tourist with a few dollars to spend could have his pick from a number of beautiful educated young women, and if he wanted to dangle the prospect of marriage and emigration his power was enormous.

And apart from the individual, and often sad, stories of each potential emigrant, there was the knowledge of the damage that emigration was doing to Cuba. I several times heard the Bishop lament that he was losing the cream of the crop: the most dedicated and faithful Catholics, who were leaving. And I had to ask myself: "What would have happened if they all decided to stay?" The Communists, in fact, would encourage or even try to force the most talented dissidents to leave. Sometimes they were quite blunt: "If you don't decide to leave for the States, you will be in prison before six months have passed." Many heroic Cubans have opted to stay even when they had the chance to leave, so that they could continue to struggle to reform their own country despite all the obstacles. I had, and still have, enormous respect for the Cuban priests and bishops who stayed. They continued serving the Church in Cuba despite enormous obstacles when they could have left at any time (The Communists would have loved to see them go) and gone to work at thriving and prosperous parishes in Florida or elsewhere.

I saw a movie called "Havana". Robert Redford plays a professional gambler in Havana during the last days of the Batista regime as the rebel forces advance. He's not interested in politics, but gets involved with the wife of a leading political activist. Anyway, there was one line that struck me. One of the characters is a bright Cuban reporter who shows Redford the ropes, and he is an admirer of Castro (who is still fighting in the hills). But he decides to move to Florida. He comments : "That's the problem with us Cubans: we all know what should be done here, but instead of doing it we go to Miami." I had much sympathy for those Cubans I knew who decided to leave, and I can't honestly criticize them for their decision. At the same time I felt the pain inside of thinking "If only you would stay *here*. There is so much you could *do*."

10

Some Happy Memories

WHEN I LOOK back on my four years in Cuba, a lot of happy memories come to mind. Each one says something about the reality of life for Cuban Catholics today, so I think I'll just share some of them without trying to organize them in any logical sequence.

—One thing that always brings a smile to my face is when I look over a few snapshots that I have of the kids who regularly showed up for the Saturday religion classes, and their volunteer teachers. So bright, so hopeful, so anxious to learn, so open to God's spirit. As far as religion was concerned, Marxist indoctrination seemed to just roll off them like water off a duck's back. They usually seemed so happy to be there, and the teachers were so proud of them, and so happy to be able to share God's word with them. Teaching materials were very limited, but the Bishop managed to photocopy some booklets for the teachers to use. There was rarely anything that we could give the kids to use or take home. But the teachers sometimes showed me what they had had to use in the harsher years of religious oppression. In those days if the religion teachers wanted a text to use, they would have to find a working typewriter, a ribbon that still had some ink on it, some paper (rare) and some used carbon paper. Then they could copy out a couple of blurry copies of a child's catechism, or some prayers or hymns. Now they were *so* grateful to have a neat printed text to use. (But they never threw away their old tattered pamphlets—or anything else—just in case.) I myself used to work each year with a little group of high-school age kids, and they so loved to be able to present what they had heard in school about religion and to be able to hear an intelligent response. The youth of Cuba fill me with great hope for the future.

—On two occasions I had the great joy of being able to arrange the visit of Fr. Augusto Seubert, an American Capuchin-Franciscan who has been working for many years in Nicaragua giving Bible courses to adult village leaders. He is an expert in the Bible, and an expert in the art of teaching the Bible. We were able to offer several serious adult Bible courses by day and by night. The participants were *so* hungry for knowledge of the Scriptures, and got a lot out of the courses. Augie was much impressed with their enthusiasm, and much impressed with their academic preparation. He had been used to teaching very intelligent farmers in Nicaragua who had never been able to attend more than a couple of years of grammar school, while in Cuba most of the participants were college graduates. He did notice two big differences, however. For one thing, his usual method was to talk about a part of the Bible, then break up the class into small groups, giving each group Bible passages to look up, read, and examine together, and then report to the whole group what they had found and what *they* thought about the texts. But they were used to the Communist education method where the students are *told* what the official doctrine is. They were astonished that they were being now asked to think for *themselves* and be open to the Spirit. He also found that when he would break up the class into random groups for the small-group discussion, his distribution was ignored and the students formed their *own* groups. Since they presumed that there were one or more police spies planted in the class, no one wanted to share their ideas unless they knew and were sure of every other member of the small group. It was so nice to see their joy at discovering the Scriptures.

—When I had my hernia operation I was sent home from the hospital the same day to recuperate. I was laid up for a few days, and I was so touched by the concern that the parish members showed for me. They made sure I had food and care, and really watched out for me. This was typical of their love for their priests. They were so happy to have us with them, and so appreciative of what little we could do for them. I had the pleasure of celebrating the 25th anniversary of my ordination as a priest while I was there, and I still have the hand-made congratulation cards they gave me (store-bought cards were an unheard-of luxury in Cuba), and I'll never know how they managed to put together food for a joyous parish celebration. I have never felt the love and affection of parish members as strongly anywhere as I did in Cuba. That's not to put down in any way the wonderful people I have served, and am serving, elsewhere. But in Cuba the bond between priest and people is very deep.

—I recall the "procession" every year for the Feast of "Our Lady of Charity of Cobre", special patroness of Cuba. The little statue of Mary holding the child Jesus which is enshrined in Cobre, near Santaigo on the eastern end of the island has long had both religious and political meaning.

The slaves who worked the copper mines there considered her their special patroness in their struggle against their owners and employers for a better life. And those who fought against Spain to try to win the independence of Cuba likewise took her as their patroness. So she came to represent both faith and freedom. So while (with rare exceptions) all outdoor religious processions were strictly forbidden in Cuba, the police were always especially alert at her Feast on Sept. 8 every year. They believed that if anti-government action would start anyplace, it would probably be at that feast.

Solution; hold the processions *inside* the churches! The church would be packed to overflowing, and at the end of Mass a replica of the statue would be carried around the inside of the building. Of course there was hardly room to move, so the "procession" was really a matter of pushing through the crowded aisles with the statue to make several circuits of the church, while everyone sang hymns and the national anthem at the top of their lungs, waving Cuban flags and throwing flowers and confetti. The energy of the crowd would practically blow the roof off the church. (An interesting aside: Ernest Hemingway lived in Cuba for years and loved it dearly. He was not religious, but came to share the Cubans' tender devotion to Our Lady of Charity of Cobre. When he won the Nobel Prize for literature he went there afterward and left his Nobel medal in thanksgiving, and there it remains to this day.)

—I remember with much joy and great admiration the young men and women who after a full Marxist education decided nonetheless to enter the Cuban national seminaries to study for the priesthood, or enter the postulancies of the different religious orders to become Sisters or Brothers. The number of vocations was growing steadily.

—We managed to get a fairly large-screen color TV and two video-players (don't ask how) and set them up in the small parish meeting room, which could seat maybe 60 people. On Saturday and Sunday nights the doors would be open to anyone who wanted to see a (free) video. Some were explicitly religious videos, which were an astonishing novelty since there was no religious programming on TV, or in the theaters. Others were just movies which had a good moral tone or message, but likewise would not be on Cuban TV. When a church managed to get hold of such a video (not always easy) we would shamelessly pirate copies for the other churches (with apologies to the copyright owners: we would have bought more originals if it had been possible to do so). People loved it, both for the content and for the intoxicating experience of watching something not approved or censored by the Party beforehand. Some films were mostly just wholesome entertainment. Others were more moving and challenging. Word would circulate on the grapevine about what we would show. I remember when we showed "Dead Man Walking" with Spanish subtitles. It is the wrenching story of Sister Helen Prejean's work with a condemned rapist and murderer before his execution, and with the families of his victims. We showed it several times, always to a packed audience. It could move you to tears, but at one showing I noticed that a whole row of watchers cried and cried and cried. Only after all had left did someone tell me that they had a family member awaiting execution for killing someone in an anti-Communist action. Anyway, it was worth the effort to make good films available. The government eventually caught on to the power of videos and when I left there were much stricter controls on the purchase or importation of video players or tapes.

—All in all, I guess that my memories of Cuba are predominantly happy because religiously everything was on the upswing despite all the limitations. Church attendance (at all Churches: Catholic, Protestant or whatever), number of baptisms, confirmations, religion class attendance, vocations, number of Bibles distributed, etc., etc.: all the statistics kept climbing and climbing (O.K., they *did* start from close to zero). So, it was a satisfying and really optimistic place to serve.

11

Some Sad Memories

—PROBABLY MY SADDEST memories of Cuba are centered around suicide. Statistics about almost every health problem and cause of death in Cuba are easy to come by because the Cuban government is very proud of its accomplishments in health care and very anxious to improve further. But there was almost total official silence on the suicide rate. I did read elsewhere that the Pan American Health Service reported that Cuba had the highest suicide rate in Latin America, and certainly my own experience as a parish priest tended to bear that out. Apart from the people whom I knew personally who committed suicide, there was the comparatively large number of people who would consult with me privately because they were struggling with very strong temptations to take their own lives. And often they were people of faith. Usually it was not a temptation toward suicide because of a terrible moment of crisis. Rather people would tell me that the day-to-day problems of the Cuban reality were just wearing them down further and further, until they felt that death would be a relief. During my first year serving in Cuba I dealt with more suicidal persons that I had in my total previous 20 years of ministry elsewhere.

The people were keenly aware of the tragic problem, even though there was almost no public reporting of it. Just about everyone had experienced suicide among their friends or family members. And sometimes when a prominent person died the word spread that it had been a suicide, even though there was no official public comment on it.

I always found that when I would preach at Mass the people were very attentive. They really wanted to hear what I had to say about the Gospel, and about life in the light of the Gospel. But any time I spoke about the topic of suicide there was absolute stillness. A priest in Cuba has to take into account that in an average Sunday congregation there will almost certainly be some people present who are, or have been, seriously thinking of suicide, and the majority of the others have known the sadness of suicide among family or friends.

I recall once on Holy Thursday, when the Church solemnly commemorates the Last Supper of Jesus, and His "Agony in the Garden", I got a request to please try to go to one of the hospitals. A nurse had tried to kill herself by soaking herself in kerosene and setting herself on fire (this was not an uncommon suicide method). She had somehow survived, but was dying slowly from the terrible burns. I managed to get to the hospital that night, despite transportation problems, and the door-keeper let me through. Most of her face had been burned away, and she could not speak. I remember the immensely tender care she was getting from the elderly nurse on duty, who spoke to her as though she were her little infant. She died the next day, Good Friday, and when we prayed for her in Church the people seemed to understand deeply the connection between her sufferings and those of Jesus.

—Another sad memory that comes readily to mind when I think of those years in Cuba is the explosion in prostitution. Prostitution had been greatly reduced by programs introduced to help the women after the success of the Revolution, but with the influx of foreign tourists and the circulation of the super-powerful dollar it had gotten worse in recent years than it had ever been.

In Santa Clara where I served it was not so evident, as fewer tourists visited there, but it was truly ugly in Havana. I would only take the train to Havana a few times a year for meetings or errands, but it became a more and more unpleasant place to walk. If you looked anything like a foreign tourist (as I certainly did) you would be approached repeatedly by prostitutes or their pimps, especially near the big hotels or the dollar stores. And while hitchhiking was an important mode of transportation for everyone, you would often see strikingly dressed young women at the corners ignoring any offers of a ride in the normal beat-up cars and waiting for the tourist cars or taxis. Year by year the age of the prostitutes got younger and younger into early high school age.

Child prostitution was spreading as well, although the government would loudly denounce it and promise to stamp it out. (Adult prostitution was generally tolerated by the police, for the revenue it brought into the country, with only the occasional sweep when it got too obvious on the streets.) I recall a tourist from Switzerland who stopped in to see me one day. He had pretty well roamed the world, and liked to walk all over in the cities. He told me that he had never seen such blatant child prostitution anywhere as he had seen in Havana, not even in Thailand. Adults would approach him on the streets offering their own kid.

The buying power of the dollars made by prostitution was tremendous in the Cuban economy. A prostitute could make in one night what a surgeon made in a month. By the time I left more and more foreign groups were organizing sex tours to Cuba exclusively to take advantage of the prostitution. As AIDS had previously been largely controlled by strict public health measures, that was one more attraction for foreigners—with the result that number of AIDS cases was once again climbing. I later saw a U.S magazine article refer to the situation as "picking the flowers of the Revolution".

Apart from the damage done to each prostitute personally as a child of God, there was also the degrading effect on the people's spirit. Even those Cubans not at all involved felt the national humiliation of seeing the cream of your young people being sold off for the pleasure of foreigners.

—My other sad memory is of the depressing effect of generalized falsehood. People so often told me how sick they were of having to pretend to believe in things they actually rejected in their hearts, and of having to silence their own true opinions. On top of that there was the general need of constantly finding ways to cheat the system in order to get by. I learned soon after arrival there that when a light bulb or florescent tube burned out in Church (we were able to replace them thanks to some dollars) it should be placed on *top* of the garbage outside. They would disappear almost instantly. For many people the only way to get a new light bulb or tube was to sneak a burned out one into work and switch it for a working one in a fixture, then sneak the good one home. Even the police, who had an excellent reputation for honesty (even among those who hated the Communist system) were having a hard time keeping clean. A "tip" in dollars to look the other way could double or triple what the cop's family could buy for the table that month. During my 20 years in Central America, bribery of police was generally the norm. In El Salvador my concern was to be protected *from* the Police, not *by* them. So it was sad to see the basic honesty of the Cuban cops getting worn down by the economic crisis.

—When Christopher Columbus first saw the Island of Cuba, he wrote in the ship's log "this is the most beautiful land that man has ever seen". The beauty of both the land and the people has been much damaged. I have many happy memories of Cuba, but these sad ones are very much present as well.

12

Uncle Sam and I

I WAS PLEASED in early 1994 when I got word that the Cuban government had granted the Church's request for a visa for me to go and do pastoral work there. Such permissions are not automatically granted. When the Cuban Bishops or Religious Superiors have foreign volunteers willing to come to Cuba, they can only present the request and let the Papal Nuncio negotiate. Only some of such requests are granted, and there is no way of knowing how many or when. Sometimes there is simply no reply for years. But once an affirmative reply is given, the foreign priest or religious order member has to get to Cuba quickly, before the entry permit expires. So, the potential volunteers have to keep themselves free from long-term commitments elsewhere and be ready to pack and move at once if the visa comes through.

So, I lost no time and flew to Cuba from Nicaragua in June of 1994, was granted a one-year residency (to be renewed annually) by the Cuban government, and was assigned by my Superiors and the Bishop as Pastor in Santa Clara. Once I was settled in, I figured I had better see what my status now was with the U.S. government. The U.S. had tried to prohibit its citizens from even traveling to Cuba, but it was hard to make such a law stick according to the Constitution. So it ended up that it was not illegal to go to Cuba, but once you bought a cup of coffee there you could be prosecuted for "trading with the enemy". (Of course, you could apply to the U.S. Treasury Department for permission to travel to Cuba for cultural, journalistic, scientific or religious purposes. If you got that permit, you could trade with the enemy without fear of prosecution by the U.S. But many U.S. citizens consider having to ask for such permission to be an unwarranted restriction of their freedom, so don't bother.)

Anyway, I first wanted to find out whether I would be able to receive donations of money or materials from family, friends and religious groups in the States under the U.S. embargo laws. So I took the train to Havana. (That's always an interesting trip. It can take days to get a ticket, and the trains are run-down and usually lacking food or water. But once you have the ticket your car and seat number is assigned and guaranteed, and once you get on you know you'll get there sooner or later, regardless of any repairs made along the way.)

After settling in at one of our Friaries in Havana, where the Spanish Capuchins were always most hospitable, I hiked over to the "U.S. Interests Section of the Swiss Embassy". This is something of a joke. Since the U.S. refuses to have diplomatic relations with Cuba, there is no U.S. "Embassy" there. Instead there is a huge well-guarded building on the most prominent of Havana's avenues where everything that an embassy does is done by American Foreign Service personnel, but officially it is an office of the *SWISS* embassy, even though the only thing Swiss there is, perhaps, some cheese in the cafeteria. The Cubans maintain a similar, but smaller, joke in Washington. As I approached the building I first had to present my papers at a Cuban Police post before being allowed to go further. Once at the gates I explained my purpose to a Cuban guard employed by the U.S. and was told to come back the next day at a certain hour. I did so, and eventually got in. I filled out a form stating my business and took a seat in a large waiting room with a few dozen other people. While we waited we could watch "TV Martí", the U.S. anti-communist propaganda station. Since the Cuban government blocks the signal, this is the only place in Cuba you can see it.

Eventually my name was called and I went to stand at the correct window to talk to a rather bored-looking U.S. Foreign Service person through thick plexi-glass. He slipped me a two-page summary of the "Trading With The Enemy" act and told me that if any person or group in the U.S. were to try to mail me more than $300 a month in donated medicines without first getting a Treasury Department License they would be subject to up to 10 years in prison and a quarter of a million dollars fine. (No, I'm not making this up.) While trying to digest this fact it occurred to me to ask him how they would know people were sending me, let's say, *two* $300-worth packages a month? He shrugged and said that no one was really keeping track. This turned out to be true. It is a law that can be used as a tool. They can slam you for breaking it, or just look the other way, according to what suits their purpose at the moment. Quite similar to the Cuban Communist system.

Over the years, this turned out to be the case. While to avoid trouble most people would send me stuff by mailing it to Canada or Spain to be re-mailed from there, other stuff came direct. Since books were "cultural" I could legally buy them by mail from the States, and they would arrive. But when I tried to buy a computer diskette of religious "clip art" to put drawings in my Parish Bulletin, the Liturgical Press of Collegeville Minnesota wrote back that it was illegal to sell electronic media to Cuba. And when the "Family Rosary Crusade" of Fr. Payton tried to send me packages of free Rosaries for my people, they were likewise rejected by the U.S. Post Office. One of my relatives (I leave her un-named lest the Feds track her down) tried to send me a box of Christmas cookies. The Post Office computer didn't know what to do with it, but after a couple of refusals she found a Post office that accepted it. She paid the postage and off it went. Later she was informed by the Post Office that the cookies were indeed illegal. They would not be delivered, nor returned to her. They are still, I imagine, in a government warehouse someplace, waiting for the fall of Castro.

Once I was back in Santa Clara, I would receive occasional friendly visits from U.S. Foreign Service people who were in the area for one reason or another, sometimes to check up on the safety of returned rafters. (U.S. diplomats could make such trips as long as they gave the Cuban government advance notice.) I always tried to receive them with the same courtesy and honesty with which I received visits from the Communist authorities, reporters or any other visitors. I always tried to give everyone honest answers, to promote dialogue and understanding. Naturally, I made sure I received the U.S. officials in public areas, with doors and windows open. Their job, of course, was to fish for information, but I have no trouble in giving honest information to anyone who asks. Sometimes they would provide me with educational stuff from the U.S. Information Agency, which I might pass on once I had filtered it for what might be judged as propaganda. There were some materials for English teachers which were much appreciated by local educators. Sometimes the visitors would pass on to me back issues of medical or dental journals, which were eagerly read by the local docs. Old U.S. newspapers were a more delicate matter. People *hungered* for outside news, but a U.S. paper could easily be classified legally as "enemy propaganda" so they were passed around discreetly until they were worn to shreds. (Even when I got packages of books from Mexico, people treasured the wrinkled sheets of Mexican newspapers used as packing material and passed them from one family to another to read.)

As there were charter flights directly between the U.S. and Cuba, I decided to ask if I might use them when I returned to the States for my annual vacation. Otherwise, I would go through Mexico or another country. The response I got from the U.S. State Department (after they consulted the Treasury Department) was fascinating. I was informed that I could fly on those direct charter flights since (as stated in their official letter to me) "the Treasury Department considers you a 'Cuban National', i.e. someone domiciled in Cuba." However, the letter went on, "you, *not the U.S. Church*, (italics added) must pay for your tickets, although you may be reimbursed later." Get it? If the U.S. Church bought my ticket (since I'm a "Cuban National") they would be "trading with the enemy".

But if *I* ("Cuban National") buy the ticket, and the Church reimburses me five minutes later, it's O.K. Beautiful.

The State Department letter then went on to inform me that "you may not receive a salary from the U.S. Church while in the United States." So if while on vacation in the States I should help in a parish, or celebrate weddings, baptisms or funerals, anyone who would *pay* me for such services would (you guessed it) be trading with the enemy (me, the "Cuban National"). But, not to discourage me too much, the letter continued, "you may draw up to $1,000 per month from a U.S. bank account while in the United States." The letter then ends with "best wishes for your continued good work."

I must admit that I was tempted to ask Cardinal O'Connor of New York to publicly buy me my ticket to return to Cuba, letting the F.B.I. and the newspapers know in advance of the place and time, just to see if they would arrest him, but I figured it was better just to ignore the whole thing. Even those who are supposed to enforce these laws seem to know that they don't make much sense. I remember the first time I flew directly to the U.S. from Cuba after a year. I had all my papers ready, prepared for interrogation at the airport. I was a bit nervous. But as we approached Immigration somebody in a uniform yelled "Everyone with U.S. Passports over here!" and then waved us past while we held our unopened passports in the air. So much for the Cuban threat to U.S. security. On another occasion the Immigration man looked at my passport and asked where I was coming from. I told him I lived in Cuba and was a pastor there. He glanced toward his supervisor, who shrugged, and in I came.

I never did ask for any license from the U.S. Treasury Department, because I thought it was unjust to require one. So, there was some financial creativity involved in getting money into Cuba for pastoral and charitable work. I more than once found myself skulking about Havana with wads of hundred-dollar bills strapped to my leg, but everything worked out fine. Some day I'll be able to thank all the people who helped me and my parish members out, but at the moment that 10 years in jail is still on the books in the U.S.

While there is some humor in the oddity of these laws and decisions, something important should be kept in mind. The reason why the Pope has so often spoken out against economic embargoes throughout the world is that they always tend to hurt the poorest and weakest people. They are aimed at dictators and oppressive regimes. But anyone with power or the right connections can get around them. It is only the poorest, the sickest and the weakest who get hurt by them, and that's why they should be lifted.

13

The Pope's Visit

AT THE TIME I arrived in Cuba in 1994, the possibility that the Pope might visit there as he had visited so many other countries had long been talked about. But it was feared that such a visit would never take place because the Pope always insists on being able to speak to the people when he visits. It seemed unlikely that the Cuban Communists, who allowed no religious expression on television or radio, would allow the Pope such access, especially given his strong statements in the past in defense of human rights.

So it came as a delightful surprise when it was finally announced that he would visit Cuba in 1998. Even more surprising were the changes that the government made in its policies in preparation for the visit. Suddenly the Church was able to obtain materials to print up great quantities of religious pamphlets, and to import even more from Mexico and elsewhere. Then we got the O.K. to actually go door-to-door throughout the island to give the literature to anyone who wanted it. A large group of volunteers got organized in my parishes. They split into teams, drew maps of all the streets, and set out knocking on doors. Unheard of! Along with the little pamphlets the Cuban Church printed up ("Who is Jesus?", "What is the Church?", "Who is the Pope?" etc) we had a <u>million</u> copies of the Gospel of Mark (printed in Mexico) to give away! The volunteers were astonished at being received so well at almost every house and apartment. Even dedicated members of the Communist Party received the materials gratefully. People would run after the volunteers to say "Wait! You missed my house! I want some!" There was a tremendous hunger for all things spiritual. The million copies of Mark's gospel were gobbled up quickly, and the Church ordered a million more (in a population of only 11 million people.) It was unbelievable.

(Even two years later, in 2000, I read a newspaper column by Cal Thomas where he flatly stated that "Bible distribution is forbidden in Cuba."

I wrote to explain that, thanks be to God, that was no longer the case. Distribution was still unfairly limited at times, but literally millions of copies had been distributed with no problems from the Communists. Some commentators refuse to acknowledge any improvement in the Cuban government's attitude and practice toward religion.)

The Bishops also obtained hundreds of thousands of big color posters. Some were of Jesus, opening His heart in love for humanity, with the phrase printed below saying "Jesus, in You I trust". Others were of the Pope, with the saying "Messenger of truth and hope." We sold them for a token price of a few pennies and many homes posted them on their outside doors and walls. Occasionally, some were torn down at night. But they were quickly replaced. Most were not bothered.

Replicas of the Statue of Mary as "Our Lady of Charity of Cobre" were made for each Diocese, and they made the rounds of every church, setting off joyful prayer-filled celebrations. (Processions were still forbidden outdoors, but as often as not "mini-processions" just happened as the statue arrived by car and was brought into the Church with all bells clanging in joy.)

But at the same time, difficult negotiations were going on about every detail of the visit. (I limit myself to what I saw where I was in Santa Clara. I didn't get to other parts of the country during that visit.) By far the most important concession that the government made was that the Pope would celebrate four huge outdoor Masses in four different cities, and that all would be broadcast live by television and radio throughout the island in their entirety and with no censorship. But there were still questions. Would workers and students get a day off to go to see the Pope? (generally, yes.) Would there be transportation for those who wished to go? (yes) Who will be invited to each Mass? Will the Communist leadership attend, and if so where will they sit? (yes, front row) Will Protestant leaders be invited? (yes, front row) Will the Masonic Lodges be invited? (Yes, and they came gladly.) Which flag will be higher, the Cuban flag or the Papal flag? (compromise: keep them apart) Etc. etc. etc.

There was a particular problem in Santa Clara, where the Pope would celebrate his first Cuban Mass. In the other cities the Masses would be celebrated in the largest open plazas, and each plaza was dedicated to some Cuban hero of the wars of independence against Spain, and dominated by a statue of the Hero. (The Pope did his homework well, and always pointed out that those Cuban heros were believers, or at least sympathetic to the spiritual). But the plaza in Santa Clara was dedicated to Che Guevara, because it was his victory over the Batista forces in battle there in 1958 that assured the victory of the Revolution. The government wanted very much for the Pope to celebrate the Mass at the foot of the huge statue of Che holding his rifle. The Bishop did not want this. Eventually it was decided to set everything up on some sports fields on the other side of the city.

But even as the materials were being distributed, and cartons of papal caps, buttons, visors and vests were being readied for the crowd-control volunteers, there was always the fear that it would not happen, or that it would be sabotaged at the last minute by the hard-line Communists (who were enraged that Fidel was allowing such a thing, even though they couldn't express publicly their disapproval.)

Then: the unbelievable happened. A few days before the Pope's scheduled arrival Fidel interrupted the evening TV programming to give a speech. That was not unusual. What was unusual this time was the length: about seven hours! About two in the morning, when even the most dedicated TV fans had gone to bed, Fidel got to his point. He said that he wanted the Pope to leave Cuba saying that his visit here had been the best visit he had ever made to any country. He said that *everyone* should pitch in and make sure that *everything* went perfectly. He urged *everyone* to attend the Pope's Masses, including Party members and committed atheists. He said that there must be no banners or placards that would in any way be offensive to the Pope. He said that no political slogans of any kind, even in favor of the Revolution, should appear or be shouted. He said that *everyone* should listen to the Pope with attention and respect, and that if anyone did not agree with what the Pope said he should keep a courteous silence and not give any type of negative response.

Over the following days Fidel's words were repeated over and over (in prime time.) The word was out, from the top. From then on everything went smoothly. Time off for workers and students, buses, trucks and trains available, courteous and efficient police guidance at every step.

I was among the priests concelebrating that first Mass with the Pope, there in Santa Clara. It was an astonishing sight. A huge crowd. Believers for the first time in their lives publicly expressing their faith in an open-air Mass without fear. Nonbelievers and the curious listening to the word of God openly. Holy and joyous songs swelling the air. Intoxicating. Then came the time for the Pope's first sermon in Cuba. His theme was the importance of marriage and the family. That might seem harmless enough. But when he got to the part about education he became more and more direct in criticizing the Cuban Communist model for leaving out spiritual values. Then he hit a sore point: the separation of kids from their parents for long stays at the government boarding schools in the countryside. (Even many Communist parents hated this, because of the dreadful moral degradation at some schools). The audience was astonished. For the first time in their lives they were hearing someone, in public, criticize the State, and he was getting away with it! Then he said it: "Don't wait for this to be *given* to you, *take up your responsibility!*" Silence. He had asked them to *change* things! Then a ripple of applause, growing louder and louder, and cheers. They could *agree* with the criticism *out loud* and not be arrested!

From then on there were more and more interruptions for applause and cheering at each papal Mass.

Some people lament that the Pope's visit didn't cause major changes in Cuban policies. I think they neglect the most important effect of his visit. People heard at last public criticism of the system, and experienced the power of publicly shouting their agreement. The toothpaste is out of the tube, and they can't get in back in now.

When the Communion time arrived at the Mass, all had been arranged in advance. During the previous weeks, all the parishes had been given little slips of paper. We told the people at Mass that anyone who usually goes to Communion on Sunday could also go to Communion at the Pope's Mass by just pinning that paper to their shirt or dress. (Just to prevent the curious from going up, not even knowing what Communion was.) But we were also given a limited number of special tickets for those who would receive Communion directly from the Pope rather than from one of the concelebrating priests. The Bishop asked that we give those tickets to the people who had never dropped out, who had persevered at Sunday Mass even during the worst times of religious repression in the past. What a sight! With the whole Communist leadership sitting in the front row watching, these mostly elderly people who had been ridiculed and despised for decades for persevering in the faith, going up to receive Communion from the Pope himself with the massed choirs of all the parishes singing at the top of their lungs!

I'll mention one other interesting point about the Pope's visit to Santa Clara. The organizers had asked each parish to recruit crowd-control volunteers to keep the huge crowds in order and keep passageways open. They had to be young and strong, able to work hard through the heat of the day. Our parish youth group provided enthusiastic volunteers, and they were delighted to get their "official" papal caps and vests! They had to be at their assigned posts at the field before dawn on the day of the Mass, to get their instructions and have everything ready before the first crowds arrived. But when my group got to their post they found that they were going to share the crowd-control duties with a contingent of the Communist Youth League! They approached each other somewhat diffidently, started to chat and broke the ice. Our kids had some cards with pictures of the Pope, and the Communist youths gratefully accepted them as gifts. Then: to work. When they got back to the parish that night, exhausted but deliriously happy, they commented that one of the most moving things about the whole day was the fact that the Pope had gotten them and the Communist Youth League to literally work hand-in-hand and arm-in-arm for the good of everybody.

I know that some observers think that Castro did all this as a master politician, just to put on a show and gain some international prestige. Perhaps. I tend to agree with those others who say that something truly spiritual was going on in Castro's soul. I hope so. In any case, the Pope's visit there was an astonishing spiritual experience for the people of Santa Clara, believers and non-believers alike.

14

Goodby to Cuba

As soon as the Pope left Cuba, the government started to make sure that everyone still knew who was in charge. People had been very excited by the Pope's visit. They had experienced unprecedented freedom of assembly and religious expression. They had seen the Pope on Cuban TV, or heard him in person, say any number of things out loud that any Cuban could be thrown in jail for saying. And some of the remarks made by Cuban Bishops on TV were so forceful that people asked out loud whether they would be prosecuted later. So as far as the Cuban leadership was concerned, it was time to tighten the screws again.

Quietly, without any publicity the Communists let individual Bishops and religious superiors know that they had to get their people to settle down, or else. Some of the hints were rather clear: refusal of expected permission for a parish to buy a car, or to buy materials to fix a roof, etc. Others were more nebulous.

It was in this atmosphere that in early 1998 I was told that it was the government's decision that I would have to leave Cuba at once. After further dialogue, that order was changed and the government decided that I could stay in Cuba a few more months, until my current one-year residency permit ran out, but that I would have to leave my parishes in Santa Clara and spend my remaining time in some parish in Havana.

As no reasons were given, there is room for speculation. As I said, the government made the decision in the context of a general tightening up of control. About 40% of the Catholic priests in Cuba are foreigners, and the Bishops depend heavily on that help. So the removal of one of the foreign priests would send a clear message to the Bishops as to what might happen if more were obliged to go. And perhaps the fact that I was the only American priest on the island might make my exclusion an expression of Cuba's disappointment at the U.S.'s failure to respond to Cuban overtures toward more friendly relations. Who knows?

But with regard to my own case, I can think of a number of particular reasons as well. The Cuban government was not pleased with the parish's meager efforts on behalf of prisoners. They didn't like our little parish Bulletin, or our study of the U.N. Universal Declaration of Human Rights, or our freely elected Parish Council, etc. They certainly didn't like the fact that I spoke honestly with foreign reporters. They were particularly upset with a well-done story by Steve Fainaru in the Boston Globe. He was a careful reporter, and after speaking with me at length he wrote his story with much concern for the possible reprisals (even checking the final text with me over the phone before publication.) It was a truthful story, and I even thought the Cuban government would be pleased that I spoke out against the U.S. embargo in a U.S. paper. But it also contained some truths about the situation in Cuba that they did not want talked about, so that upset them.

Any mention of Cuban prisoners of conscience is, of course, absolutely intolerable to them.

Anyway, our response was to accept the Party's decision in silence. To protest would have been useless, and probably would have brought heavier reprisals against the Church. In any case, a foreigner has no "right" to demand to stay in a host country. But then things changed somewhat. I was advised that the Party had given instructions to put out a dis-information campaign on the street: to spread the rumor that the reason for my departure was because I had some sort of problem with the Bishop. This, of course, was a lie. So, while still not protesting my exclusion from

Cuba I made it clear to the parish members and to anyone else who asked that my departure was not my will, nor the will of the Bishop, nor the will of my religious superiors, but was entirely the decision of the Communist party of Cuba. The Party denied this (and probably will still deny it with a straight face if asked) but I decided to simply tell the truth.

At first I was ready to just move to Havana and continue to do pastoral work there until my residency permit ran out. But it soon became clear that as long as I stayed in Cuba, a number of "difficulties" would come up for the Church and for my Religious Order. As the Party controls everything, they can make life easier or make life much more difficult if they wish, without having to do anything public. So I decided to leave Cuba before my time was up, to let the others get on with their important service without being hindered by my presence.

The people in the parishes, of course, understood just how the system works. It's a tribute to them that some seriously considered mounting a public demonstration in my favor in front of Party headquarters. I talked them out of it. It would only have put them in jail, perhaps for years, and not accomplished anything. They expressed much appreciation for my having been with them, and much love. There were tears at the farewell Mass, Easter of 1998, including my own.

While I have sincerely loved the people in all the places where I have had the privilege to serve (and love the people I serve now), I must say that my love for the Cuban people is something special. Maybe because of what we went through together, maybe because we hit it off so well. An incident comes to mind—nothing of great importance, just a very strong memory that I will share here.

We had a nice parish youth group, mostly teen-agers. They gave each other a lot of support as believers in an often unencouraging environment. Once a year the Diocese organized a get-together out in the country-side for all the parish youth groups. They would spend the day in sports, song, prayer, discussion and a big out-door Mass. (That was unusual. The government ordinarily forbade any Mass outside of a Church building.) They really looked forward to it. On the appointed day they all gathered early in the morning outside church to leave together. They had pooled all the bicycles they could get so as to be able to all go, as it was a good ways out of town, even though it meant two or even three on each bike. Being teens, there naturally was much jockeying to see which guy would get to give which girl a ride on his bike, or vice versa. I wasn't going with them as I had parish stuff to do that day, but I went out to see them off. They were a great bunch of kids, and it was nice to see them all enthused about the day's activities. But as they were getting organized the mother of one of the boys showed up because he had forgotten to take his jacket. He, of course was *mortified*! Here he is trying to impress the girls and his *mother* shows up to insist he take a jacket! Egad! Anyway, she was smart enough to see that she had embarrassed him, so she backed off promptly and the two of us strolled off to the side as the kids got organized to leave. They piled onto the bikes and wobbled off uncertainly into the heavy truck and bus traffic going by. They looked so vulnerable setting off like that, so easy to fall and be crushed. I guess I saw their spiritual journey the same way. Anyway, both the mom and I resisted the temptation to yell out something dumb like "be careful!" or "watch out for the trucks!" They were on their own, filled with confidence.

It occurred to me that what I was feeling inside for those kids was not unlike what that mom was feeling: a tender love and concern for her son, hopeful yet fearful for him. I didn't just love those kids as "my flock", I loved them as my kids.

Later when I had left Cuba for good I realized that what I was feeling was not just the sadness of moving on from one happy assignment to another one. I was mourning the loss of a family that I had come to love very dearly.

When I look back on my four years in Cuba I have to ask myself if I should have done anything differently. Maybe if I had kept quiet about human rights and passed up the chances to do a little about the situation, they wouldn't have bounced me out. Maybe. But I rather think that if I failed there it was in not speaking out *enough* to protest both what the

Cuban Communists were doing and what the United States was doing. In any case, I still miss those folks deeply. I hope that what I have written in these pages will do some good. The Pope said toward the end of his visit to Cuba: "The world should open itself to Cuba, and Cuba should open itself to the world."

The more the true situation in Cuba is known, both the good and the bad, the better the chances of keeping the good and eliminating the bad. And as Americans we need to know the truth, not the propaganda from either side, if we're going to get our government to do the right thing.

—*fin*—

Father Sullivan was born in New York City in 1945. He entered the Capuchin Franciscan Order right after high school in 1963 and was ordained a priest in 1971. From 1971 to 1974 he served as a hospital chaplain and parish priest in New York and then left for Spanish language studies in Mexico and Bolivia. He served in Honduras from 1975 until 1988 in parish work and the training of lay leaders. From 1988 to 1991 he served in Nicaragua and then in El Salvador until 1994, when he was assigned to Cuba. After his involuntary departure from Cuba in 1998 he served in parish ministry and prison chaplaincy in New York and New Hampshire until being assigned to the Hispanic apostolate in Okinawa, Japan in 2005. He presently (2012) continues his ministry in Okinawa. He can be contacted by e-mail at PSofmcap@aol.com or by mail at Capuchin Friars, 1 Oroku, Naha, Okinawa, 901-0152, Japan.